REVIVAL SECRETS

Stories Told by

SAMUEL ROBINSON

&

LUC NIEBERGALL

Revival Secrets

Copy Editor: Sarah Reimer

ISBN: 9798697414972

Printed in Canada

CONTENTS

FOREWORD
By: Bill Johnson

Revival is the heart of God made manifest. It is the poor in spirit who get the privilege of experiencing both His heart and His kingdom. *Revival Secrets* is a powerful compilation of what happens when the human heart reaches such a place of hunger for the person of Jesus that nothing else will satisfy. When we are exposed to the glory of His presence, everything within us rises to proclaim, "This is why I'm alive." I encourage you to not only read this book, but to prayerfully approach each chapter, remembering that our Lord is no respecter of persons. What He does for one, He wants to do for all—every person, every nation, and every generation.

We were born to experience the fullness of revival and in turn, see the world transformed for the honour of the name of Jesus.

Bill Johnson
Bethel Church, Redding, CA
Author of "The Way of Life"
& "Born for Significance"

INTRODUCTION
By: *Samuel Robinson*

We are living in times of revival. God is encountering hearts throughout the earth. He is healing the sick and freeing the oppressed. He is transforming cities and shaking nations.

He is marking generations.

I don't believe the book you're reading came from the ambition of man; I believe it came from God's desire. I say that, because the idea for this book all came from a dream. It wasn't too long ago, when I went to sleep one evening; this was when I had a dream that shook me to my very core.

In this dream, I saw Jesus standing before me. It's one of the few times He has come to me in such a way. His face beamed with a smile, like a father looking at his son or daughter. Even though He radiated joy, I could feel the seriousness of what was occurring. Reaching out his hands, I saw that He was holding something. It was a book.

I reached out, my hand gripping the book. For a moment, He and I both held it. Even though it wasn't large per se, I could feel its weight. I could feel its importance.

The title read: "Revival Secrets."

At that point, Jesus said, "Samuel, this is a very precious gift. I'm entrusting you to have this book written. This book is no ordinary book; it is going to be an inheritance for generations who come after you."

His words carried tremendous weight. Holding the book, I experienced a part of God that I had never really experienced before; the Father's heart for generations. I found myself thinking about how His heart for revival was never for it to just be an event. It was never meant to last for only one generation. As I thought about this, it felt as though He was saying, "I'm entrusting you to have something written that will outlast you. It will bless people to believe me for revival in their generation."

I believe the heart of this book is Proverbs 13:22, which says, "A good *man* leaves an inheritance to his children's children…" This is what burns in the heart of the Father. He desires for us to leave a spiritual inheritance and legacy for the generations who come after us. This means that our experiences with God become their launching pad. When we think generationally, those who are upcoming get to have a head start.

When I think about my own life, I'm thankful that I had the benefit of having a loving father who believed that his ceiling would become my floor; that I could stand on his shoulders. My dad built his life like a man who was going to leave a legacy for his child. I believe it's important for us to understand that what we are doing here on the earth shouldn't be about necessarily building ministry, but instead about building legacy. It's in God's heart that no matter what we do, we will always have the next generations in mind.

Since this was modelled to me, I notice this with my own kids. I often think to myself, "What is the inheritance and platform that I will sow into my children?" God works generationally; and I know He has called my kids to take things where I won't be able to. As their father, I need to allow my life to be their launching pad. This is the heart of this book. We have gathered fathers and mothers who have experienced revival. We also have those who are currently experiencing new cutting-edge expressions of revival. We have brought fathers and mothers; sons and daughters together in this book for the sake of training and equipping those who will one day carry the torch.

For this book, we have asked each of them to share their stories of revival. We did this because we believe in the power of testimony. We have asked them to offer their keys and revelation because we believe in the power of impartation. Revelation 19:10 says, "Worship God! For the testimony of Jesus is the spirit of prophecy." This means that when we testify of what Jesus has done, we are giving others the opportunity to experience to some degree the same thing. Those in this book aren't testifying of what they've heard about; they are testifying of what they've seen. What they testify is a prophetic declaration of what generations coming after us can experience. Every person in this book carries a spiritual inheritance that I believe is transferable through the stories and revelation they share.

With the stories and revelations documented in this book, we have an opportunity to position ourselves in humility and teachability to learn from those who have gone before us. My heart is that everyone who reads this book will be equipped to experience revival for themselves in everyday life. What God has done, is doing, and will still do, is so much grander than any one individual. It requires all of us. It requires generations.

God has called you to be a voice of revival in your generation.

JOHN ARNOTT

John and Carol live in the Greater Toronto Area. They have four adult children, five grandchildren, and three great-grandchildren. John and Carol founded Catch the Fire Partners Network of Churches. As international speakers, they have become known for their ministry of revival in the context of the Father's saving and restoring love. They have seen millions of lives touched and changed through God's power and Christ's love. John and Carol founded a church called Toronto Airport Christian Fellowship (TACF), now known as Catch the Fire Toronto, where a sovereign outpouring of the Holy Spirit came. Catch the Fire Toronto was brought to the world's attention as a place where God was meeting with His people. John is known for his teachings on the Father's love, grace, forgiveness, and the Holy Spirit's power. He continues to impart wise counsel and provides a strong framework for those who want to see the power of God manifest in their church.

"God loves you just the way you are, so come as you are. However, God loves you too much to leave you the way you are. He's going to build in you an inward journey that will result in you going from glory to glory."

— John Arnott

A Birthing of Revival
By: John Arnott

From our perspective, our "yes" to God may at times seem small, like a mustard seed; but we would be amazed if we knew what He can do with that. Our "yes" to Him changes absolutely everything. It positions us for encounter; it positions us for transformation. It's in this place of being yielded where God can use us to reach generations. It's in this place that He can raise us up to see the masses impacted.

I went to Israel for the first time in 1974. At that point in my life I was working in business, yet having what felt like a relentless heart to know the Lord. I remember the anticipation leading up to this trip. I couldn't believe I was about to visit the *Promised Land*. I spent much time praying, doing a three-week water fast leading up to the trip. I wasn't going to Israel for any little reason; I was hungry for reality. I wanted to meet with God.

There was a minister at the conference in Israel at the time named David du Plessis. In going to this man's sessions, I had no clue what awaited me. From the stage, he talked about the love of God from John 17. However, he did it in such a way that it deeply moved me. It wasn't like previous sermons I'd heard; there was power in his words as he spoke about Jesus. I sat, listening as this revelation of love took root deep inside my heart. It completely wrecked me. I was weeping, totally undone. I couldn't get it together because I was so moved by his message of love. In the nighttime after being in these meetings, I couldn't sleep because it felt like waves of heaven were rolling over me. This happened night after night. I probably only got five or six hours of sleep in the whole week we were in Israel. These waves of heaven felt so intense that I remember praying, saying, "God if one more wave comes over me like this, I don't think I'll live through it..."

This trip without a doubt changed my life. My heart's desire was fulfilled; I knew that I met with God. After encountering the Lord so powerfully on that trip, all I could bring myself to do was pray, continuing my pursuit to know God.

Carol and I were married on a glorious June day in 1979. In 1980 we took a month trip to visit the Indonesian revival. It was absolutely lifechanging. God used us to bless them, but we were wrecked by their radical love.

On our way home, we were both in tears. We prayed, saying to God, "Lord, we don't want to give our lives to business. We have to go into the ministry. Please open doors. We will do anything for you."

Immediately, God spoke back, saying, "Good. I want you to go to Carol's hometown in Stratford Ontario and start a Charismatic church there."

We knew there were Evangelical churches and one Pentecostal church in Stratford, but there wasn't a Charismatic one. That said, we went and started our church. The Lord began visiting us in our meetings; He began blessing what we were putting our hands to. It was amazing to see how the young people in particular were coming out and encountering the Lord. Many of them were saved at our church. In all honesty, we didn't really feel like we knew what we were doing. We just kept talking about Jesus and He kept falling upon hearts. As a result of the encounter I had with the love of God in Israel, Carol and I knew we wanted a *love* church. We had an undeniable taste of love. What we didn't know was that God didn't want us to only have a *taste*; He wanted us to have a feast. He wanted us to have a true revelation of love.

At that time, word was going around about a particular man who travelled the world speaking at churches. Quickly people began saying to us, "You need to have this *Jack Winter* into your church. He's an international speaker who talks about the Father heart of God."

To be honest, I didn't know what they were talking about. I knew many itinerant speakers, but I hadn't heard of Jack Winter. Not only that, but I couldn't comprehend that someone would travel, speaking about the Father's heart. I had a theology of love; I had a taste of it. I knew it in my mind, but I didn't know God as a loving Father. My stereotype perspective of the Father was, "Watch your step, boy, or you're going to get it…"

Going with the recommendation of others, we had Jack Winter come to our church. I quickly learned that he was a wonderful man, full of kindness and compassion. As he stood behind the pulpit, he began reading from

John 14:2-6, which says, "'In My (Jesus) Father's house are many mansions; if *it were* not *so,* I would have told you. And if I go and prepare a place for you, I will come again and receive you to Myself; that where I am, *there* you may be also. And where I go you know, and the way you know.' Thomas said to Him, 'Lord, we do not know where You are going, and how can we know the way?' Jesus said to him, 'I am the way, the truth, and the life. No one comes to the Father except through Me.'"

After reading the verses, Jack looked at us, saying, "So, where is it that we are going?"

There was a quiet pause from those of us listening.

From the front row, I finally spoke up, saying, "We're going to heaven."

Another said, "We're going to eternity."

Jack smiled, saying, "Yes, but Jesus also said that through Him, we are going to the Father."

I'm not going to lie to you, for a brief moment, I didn't know if I wanted to go to the Father. I thought, "You mean we're going to go to the Father—to the one who is going to put us under the microscope? We are going to go to the one who is going to show us all of the things that are wrong with us? I don't want to do that…"

Don't get me wrong, I was happy to go to heaven; I was happy to be with Jesus. I was happy to be in eternity with Paul, Peter, and James. However, my perception of the Father was as though He was the *great light* in the distance that we should stay far away from at all costs.

Here I was as a young man, fearful of the Father, yet I found out that He is my destination. Jack kept unpacking the passage to us, now reading from John 14:11, which says, "Believe Me (Jesus) that I *am* in the Father and the Father in Me, or else believe Me for the sake of the works themselves."

This was when the penny started dropping for me. Jesus came as a man, but the Father—through the power of the Holy Spirit—works through Him. So, when Jesus heals a leper, He is saying, "This is actually the Father doing it." I began understanding the Father's heart. The Father wasn't distant. He longs to show us His amazing love for us. He longs to heal the brokenhearted and to free us from sickness and pain. He longs for us to know that we have a place in His heart.

As I would see these young men and women around the church, I would remember being a much younger believer. I got so used to hearing preaching that was full of rebuke. It was all about *doing more, praying more, studying more, giving more, and witnessing more.* I got ahold of Kathryn Kuhlman's book called "I Believe in Miracles." This led me to begin listening to her radio broadcast. It was so different from anything I'd heard. It reminded me of the heart behind Jack Winter's message. It wasn't some preacher beating us up with the Bible; it was someone drawing us into the love of the Father. It was about bringing healing to those in need. It sounded so good to me. This was what I wanted to model for the people who God brought around us. After encountering the Father's love for me, I knew I needed to show people His heart for them.

We always told those who came out to our Stratford church, "God loves you just the way you are, so come as you are; however, God loves you too much to leave you the way you are. He's going to build in you an inward journey that will result in you going from glory to glory.

That inward journey will take you on an upward journey closer to the heart of heaven. It will lead you on an outward journey to impact the world."

While pastoring this church, we learned so much about the love and power of God. We learned about hearing His voice. All these young people who were gathered around us, we taught them everything we knew. We taught them how to minister and how to pray for one another. Pressing into the Lord together resulted in Him falling upon us in supernatural ways. At the time, we were very aware of the ministry of Kathryn Kuhlman and other ministries who moved in such power, but this wasn't something we were used to. When we pressed into His power, He began to move. It was so intense. God would show up in such radical ways where I began to get worried that it seemed too out of order. It scared us at times.

It finally got to the point where one day while speaking, I said, "I don't want any of you praying for each other from now on. Carol and I will do all of the ministry. From now on, we will be the ones praying for everyone."

What I didn't realize was that I had just made a horrible mistake.

All it took was about two weeks, and the Holy Spirit gradually stopped falling upon people at our church. I remember thinking to myself, "What have I done...?"

Once the Holy Spirit stopped encountering people, I remember one time while praying. I said, "Lord, I've made a terrible mistake. Please forgive me. If you ever give us another opportunity, we want the Holy Spirit to do what He wants to do."

Being as faithful as we could be in running our church in Stratford, I vowed in my heart that I would try my best to never grieve the Holy Spirit again. It wasn't long before God began placing Toronto on our heart. In 1988, we planted a small church right by the Toronto airport. What may have seemed like a small leap of faith to some was actually the catalyst of God positioning us for something remarkable. We had no clue at the time what God was aligning us for. Carol and I longed for revival; we had tasted what it felt like for the Holy Spirit to pour out from our Stratford days.

When Carol and I started in Toronto, we wanted to be completely free to just run and do the task at hand. We wanted revival; yet, we found ourselves quickly hitting opposition. We wrestled with a lack of finances. We didn't see the anointing we thought we should see. I can remember having an intense time of prayer one day. I was saying to the Lord, "God what's the deal? We're struggling because of lack. We are hitting opposition…"

It didn't take me long to realize what God was doing within us. We began to understand that the Lord's purpose isn't just to win the lost, even though it is His will that all should come unto repentance. It isn't only His will that people would be healed; although He wants to heal. He has a plan and a purpose to mold, shape, and form us into the image of His Son. As God is raising people up to steward revival, there is an internal work that needs to take place.

Romans 8:28-32: "And we know that all things work together for good to those who love God, to those who are the called according to *His* purpose. For whom He foreknew, He also predestined *to be* conformed to the image of His Son, that He might be the firstborn among many brethren. Moreover whom He predestined, these He also called; whom He called, these He also justified;

and whom He justified, these He also glorified."

He has predestined each of us to be conformed to look like Jesus. God had commissioned us into a time of growth that would set us up for what God was going to ask us to steward. I began to understand the parable that was spoken by Jesus in Matthew 7:24-27, which says, "Therefore whoever hears these sayings of Mine, and does them, I will liken him to a wise man who built his house on the rock: and the rain descended, the floods came, and the winds blew and beat on that house; and it did not fall, for it was founded on the rock. But everyone who hears these sayings of Mine, and does not do them, will be like a foolish man who built his house on the sand: and the rain descended, the floods came, and the winds blew and beat on that house; and it fell. And great was its fall."

The key to this parable is that the rain and floods came down on both houses. The rain came; but because the one was built on the rock; because of that, it withstood the opposition. It withstood the testing. God tests and trains us, so we can remain standing. Not only will we be equipped to stand when the rains of opposition come, but we will also know how to stand when the rain of renewal comes. We will be able to stand because we've allowed our lives to be built upon Jesus. We wanted God to touch down again; we wanted to know how to keep standing when He did. We needed to embrace our time of testing and training. That was when God spoke to us.

He said, "If you're serious about wanting revival, then I want you to do two things: commit your mornings to prayer and interact with those who are anointed."

We threw ourselves into these two things. We cancelled our morning appointments and dedicated those mornings to the Lord. In these times, we would pray and study the word of God together. We fell so in love with Jesus during this time. He told me so many precious things during this time. At one point, I remember saying to Him, "I'm so sorry I come to you with my prayer lists, Lord. I'm sorry I come to you will all of my needs. I don't want that to be my prayer life. I just want to fall in love with you. I want to connect heart to heart with you."

I will never forget what He said back to me. He said, "Many people want to marry me for my money."

That cut me like a sword. It never occurred to me about how many people build a relationship with God to get something.

I cried out, saying, "Oh God, I don't want to marry you for your money. I want to marry you for you."

Carol and I threw ourselves into knowing the Holy Spirit more. We threw ourselves deeper into the Father's love. We didn't want Him in order to *get something*; we wanted Him for Him. As we did, we also began connecting with those who God had anointed for revival, inviting many of them to come to our church to minister. It wasn't long after when we decided to visit Argentina. Word was, that revival was shaking the nation.

At this time in our lives, it was a huge financial cost for us to do this trip; however, we knew we needed to go. Considering it transformed our lives, I'm thankful to this day that we paid attention to the Holy Spirit's nudging.

Arriving in Argentina, revival was rampant. We visited many places where God was undeniably moving. One of those places was a maximum-security prison that had received a touch from God. All of the prisoners were on fire for Jesus. Walking into the prison, I was dumbfounded. We expected to hear shouting and swearing; yet that wasn't what we heard at all. Instead, the prisoners were singing. In the confines of their jail cells, prisoners were singing, "I'm free! I'm free!"

How could this not move your heart to want more of Jesus? Making our rounds throughout Argentina, experiencing everything that God was doing, we had heard of a man named Claudio Friezen. We knew it would be a missed opportunity if we didn't sit under his ministry. Going to his meeting, we experienced an amazing outpouring of the presence of Jesus. At the end of the service, Claudio graciously agreed to pray for all of the foreigners who flew in to experience what God was doing in Argentina.

Carol and I waited with anticipation for our turn to be prayed for. We wanted a touch from God so badly. When Carol was prayed for by Claudio, God's presence slammed down upon her. It was almost as though she went one way and her shoes went the other! She was completely undone, laughing uncontrollably. She couldn't walk; she couldn't talk. When I was prayed for, compared to Carol I felt like God was a lot gentler with me. I fell down quietly, but God wasn't done with me.

When I got back up on my knees, I prayed in my heart, saying, "God, we are just so hungry for you…"

Right as I prayed, Claudio turned to me, saying, "Do you want it?!"

Politely, I said, "Yes." Although, in my mind I was thinking, "Why do you think we've flown thousands of miles and spent thousands of dollars to be here?"

He said, "Then take it!"

Even though these seem like simple words, they were completely transformative to me. I had never considered that the Holy Spirit was there for the taking. I always thought that we were supposed to wait passively and when the Holy Spirit was ready, He would fall upon us. I realized in this moment that our relationship with the Holy Spirit is like a divine romance where two people need to move closer together because they want each other. This truth revolutionized my relationship with the Holy Spirit. When the Holy Spirit meets someone who is hungry and thirsty for Him, we become irresistible to Him. The Lord was wanting a relationship with me, but I needed to reach back to Him.

Right when Claudio said to me, "Take it!" the Holy Spirit spoke to me. He said, "I've been trying to give this to you for years, will you take it now?"

Boom! In a split second came this reality that something had just happened to me that would change me forever.

Coming home from Argentina, we knew something was different. On the airplane ride back home, Carol led two people to the Lord. Something had changed within us. The power of God was evident. Awareness of the presence of God was increasing in our church meetings. Our hunger was greatly amplified. Some of our friends at the time told us about another man who had been touched similarly to us by the Holy Spirit in a Dr. Rodney Howard-Browne meeting. That man's name was Randy Clark.

I called Randy and we immediately hit it off. We connected so well. He loved the Lord and was hungry for the kingdom just like we were. Near the end of 1993, I said, "Randy, I need you to come to Toronto to minister at our church."

Randy said, "The earliest I can come is in January of 1994."

Leading up to January, the Holy Spirit was beginning to move more and more. People were being healed. People were falling under the power of God. Carol and I remembered what happened back in Stratford. We remembered what it was like when the Holy Spirit would slam down and transform lives in an instant. We wanted God to move like that again so badly, but found ourselves almost afraid to hope for it again. At the time, we didn't have the faith to say, "This is it! Let's go for it!" As a matter of fact, neither did Randy.

In January, Randy came to Toronto. I remember him saying, "I'm going to speak at your church, but I really don't know if anything is going to happen. It's only happened once before when God poured out so dramatically."

We replied, "Let's just step out in faith together and see what God does."

I remember the night of January 20 in 1994 so well. We were all at our church and there were about one hundred thirty people in the sanctuary. Randy stood on the stage, sharing his testimony about how one touch from God set him free from depression. He talked about the love of God and the heart of the Father. As Randy shared, everything was normal. No one laughed, shook, or even made a sound.

At the end of his message, he said, "If you would like prayer, I would be happy to lay hands on you and to pray for you."

People were hesitant at first, but they eventually decided to go to the front to get prayer. As people stood from their seats to come to the front, that's when *it* happened.

Boom!

The Holy Spirit fell.

Without people even having time to walk to the altar, it was like a bomb went off in the room. In a moment, everyone was on the floor. Some were laughing; others were shrieking. Some were yelling; others were weeping. People were under the chairs, between the rows, and in the aisles.

I was up at the front thinking, "What in the world is going on here?" I was used to seeing people fall over one at a time in ministry lines, but this was like nothing I'd ever experienced! No one did anything, no one said anything; God just crashed in on the room.

There was a huge uproar rising in the room. I had never seen or heard anything like that before in my whole life. It was gloriously chaotic. It was loud. It was full of joy. It was full of passion and expression. We undeniably knew it was God, we just didn't know why He would choose to show up like this. No one thought a move of God would look like this. People were rolling on the ground and speaking in tongues. People were so touched that emotional trauma from childhood would lift off them. Some people were so touched by the power of God that they couldn't walk and would need to be carried out. It seemed so disorderly compared to what we were used to, but heaven was all over what was taking place.

What we weren't aware of, was that this was our beginning. This was the birthing of a movement.

We extended the meetings to the next night, and then the next. People kept coming and the Holy Spirit kept showing up.

I said, "Randy you can't go home... Can we call your wife to see if you can stay longer?"

We called Randy's wife and said, "Can Randy stay a bit longer? God is moving!"

She graciously replied, "Yes, Randy can stay for two more days."

Those two days passed but God poured out even more powerfully.

We called Randy's wife back again, saying, "Randy can't go back home yet... Can he stay longer please? You wouldn't believe what God is doing!"

She laughed, replying, "Fine, Randy can stay two more days, but after that I want my husband back!"

Word kept spreading about what God was doing. People would say things like, "My marriage was healed. My body was healed. My pain is gone. My shame is gone." People began getting healed from all sorts of things. They were healed of mental, emotional, and physical issues. The testimonies seemed endless! We knew that this was the move of God we had been dreaming and praying for.

When Randy finally went home, Carol and I knew it was up to us to try and steward what God was doing. In moments like these, people often assume they will be full of faith; when really, it's in these moments when we often battle with our own inadequacies. We wrestle with our own unworthiness. At the time, we weren't in touch with the anointing that was over our own lives.

To say we were praying panic prayers would be an understatement. My greatest fear was this: what if I go up on the stage and greet everyone, but the Holy Spirit doesn't show up? Thankfully, God covers our shortcomings. All He's looking for are people who have a booming "yes" in their heart. When Carol and I went up on that stage—when we were on our own—the Holy Spirit came in the same way He had been coming all that time.

When word spread about what God was doing, thousands flocked to the church. People would line up outside at 3 PM for the doors to open at 7 PM. The healings, signs, and wonders kept increasing. The manifestations of the Holy Spirit continually surprised us. At times, it felt like our theology was scrambling, trying to keep up with what the Holy Spirit was doing.

We started taking a lot of heat and persecution for what God was doing. Many were offended, but to me, this is a very small price considering what we received. Many people would say the move of God couldn't have been from Him because it was so disorderly. After all, it's not an overstatement to say that people were disorderly in how they would encounter Him. Some who would rise up against what God was doing would say things like, "One of the fruits of the Spirit is self-control, so this can't be from God."

We need to understand something: we receive the fruit of self-control so we can control ourselves, not so that we can control the Spirit of God. When He comes upon us, our best move is to yield to Him. We can get so caught up with the manifestations. For me, I'm not as interested in whether someone laughed, fell, or shook. I'm interested in knowing what Jesus did in their heart during that touch from Him. Did they encounter the loving Father through what took place? Did they become more passionate about seeing their family saved? Did they fall more in love with Jesus? If so, then I'm so glad God encountered them in such a dramatic way.

When people came to our church, it didn't matter if they were Pentecostal, Catholic, Methodist, Baptist, or anything in between. One of the most fascinating things to me was that this was so contagious. There were times when people would come to be with us for three days. When they would go home, the Holy Spirit would fall in their church the same way He was moving in Toronto! The anointing that was being poured out is now known as the *Toronto Blessing.*

We recently had our twenty-five-year anniversary of the outpouring that began on January 20 of 1994. When we think of twenty-five years going by, I'm astounded to see that what God did back then is still continuing. It's still raging, cooking, and burning. People ask me how it has lasted for so long. I honestly don't know; I wish I had a concrete answer. We've allowed our passion for Jesus to burn. We love the works of God, and Jesus loves that we love it. I don't believe that revival is ever supposed to end.

I remember when we were first overwhelmed with revival in 1994, the Lord spoke to me saying, "This is a revival that will never end."

I'm not trying to sound presumptuous in sharing this. What I believe was meant by what He said, was that this move of God is going to keep spreading, impacting, and transforming lives. The flame of it will be burning somewhere until Jesus comes back. I want people to catch that flame and to keep it burning in their heart. That flame is never supposed to go out.

Carol and I look back at everything that has happened, knowing it has been a great highlight of our lives; but we know there are greater things yet to come. Matthew 5:6 says, "Blessed *are* those who hunger and thirst for righteousness, for they shall be filled." This is where we need to ask ourselves a question: how hungry are we for Him? How thirsty are we for Him? How loud is the "yes" within in our heart?

We have seen millions of lives touched through this move of God. A movement that has touched millions, all began with God coming and visiting one hundred thirty people during an evening service. This movement started with a small church in Toronto by the airport. It started with an adamant "yes" for more of God.

— *John Arnott*

PATRICIA KING

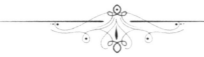

Patricia is a respected apostolic and prophetic minister, an inventive entrepreneur, a spiritual mentor, and a true mother in the faith. She is committed to loving God, loving people, and advancing the Kingdom through media, missions, events and outreach. Patricia King Ministries promotes the character and nature of Jesus Christ through the in-dwelling grace of Holy Spirit. She believes God's light belongs in the darkness, shining the life and hope of Jesus to those who long to know Him.

"When we lay ourselves down on the altar before the Lord, He can do remarkable things through us. God—plus nothing—equals everything we will ever need."

— Patricia King

Longevity in Revival
By: Patricia King

You were made for revival. God wants to invite you on a supernatural journey with Him where He will blow your mind with His goodness and His glory. He has created you to see people healed, saved, and delivered; that signs, wonders, and miracles would follow you. This is what you were created for; this is who you are.

I've had the amazing honour of witnessing several outpourings and revivals. One of them was the great outpouring of the Spirit of God that took place in Canada in 1994. This outpouring was like a portal of the supernatural that opened up and spread to the nations. There was an amazing manifestation of the glory of God. There were signs and wonders; undeniable healings and deliverances took place. This was an outpouring that shook everything. It called the lost into the kingdom of God; it in many ways woke up the church.

At that time, I was living in Mission, British Columbia. We had all heard of what was taking place in Toronto and we wanted to put on a few meetings of our own where we would seek the presence of God. We called these meetings "Wind and Fire."

I distinctly remember the very first night. During worship, we were lost in God's presence and there was an unusual sign and wonder that transpired. A specific fragrance came into the building; it was a fragrance that smelled like fire. This fragrance was so strong that the janitor of the building went around trying to locate the source of the smell, but couldn't find anything! There was no natural fire; it was the fire of the Holy Spirit.

That night there was a group of young people whose parents told them they needed to come to at least one night of the revival meetings. These kids sat at the back of the church with their arms folded, unengaged. It was clear that they didn't want to be there. On that first night, there was so much anointing released that one of the elders of the church got hit by the power of God. This resulted in him being completely undone and *drunk in the Spirit*. Being "drunk in the Spirit" is a state where we are so full of Holy Spirit that we are no longer in touch with our flesh. This is when we are full of God's joy and are experiencing a euphoric sense of His glory.

This church elder was so lost in an encounter with God that he was literally rolling up and down the aisles! Not only was he being impacted, but other people were falling down all over the place under the power of God. People were getting healed and set free right, left, and centre. These young people, previously disinterested, saw all of this and immediately ran up to the front to get a better look at what was taking place. These youth got completely blasted in the Holy Spirit. The ones who didn't yet know Jesus, gave their hearts to Him right then and there.

These revival nights were only supposed to last for a few days of meetings, but it turned out to be three solid weeks, non-stop. Every single night, God would show up in power. Our whole city was completely changed by this; in fact, it has never been the same since. This was the beginning of a few years of outpouring in our area. We began noticing that everything we put our hands to was accelerated. Just a few months after the outpouring, we were able to purchase property where we then planted a church, as well as an apostolic training centre. We sent teams to minister across Canada. This outpouring resulted in us doing revival meetings every single day—except one—for three years straight.

We tried our best to be open to the Holy Spirit, to submit ourselves to however He wanted to move. People would come from all over to be a part of what God was doing. It was amazing to see that no matter what we did, the Spirit would always fall.

Being a part of an outpouring like this was such an honour. To be a part of seeing the Lord move like this— seeing so many lives transformed—is a great privilege. It felt like we were living under a portal from heaven; like we were continually engulfed by God's glory.

Another outpouring that I was a part of took place when I was quite young. I was in my mid-thirties at the time. Even though I'm almost seventy now, this was probably one of my absolute favourite times of my life.

I was on a missions trip in a city called Tijuana, which is a border city in Mexico. At that time, eighty percent of its population lived in dire poverty. Many lived in cardboard shacks; others lived in hovels. It was so tragic seeing the state these people were living in. My heart broke for these precious people. Not only that, but I could feel God's heart breaking for them as well.

The Lord spoke to me, saying, "I want to impact Tijuana. I want you to start an outreach centre. Bring my light into the darkness."

I had never done anything like planting an outreach centre before. To do something so grand felt foreign to me. I went back to my leaders and told them what the Lord had spoken to me.

They replied, saying, "Patricia, we feel like the Lord is on this, but we don't have any money to fund this. If you go through with this, you're going to have to do everything by faith."

In going to them, I wasn't expecting finances; all I wanted was their blessing. I wanted the green light, so that I could run with what was stirring in my spirit. I immediately went into fasting and prayer. The Lord kept prompting me to move forward with what He had spoken to me. I contacted several young people that I knew between the ages of eighteen and twenty-two who were on fire for the Lord.

I said to them, "Would you want to come to Tijuana with me to plant an outreach centre? I have no money to offer you. It's going to be an adventure of faith. Together, we will bring light into the darkness."

Every single one of them responded to me with a resounding, "Yes!"

Each of us put in what money we had to help fund the project, which totaled a whopping $1,200. Here we were, a group of young people planning on starting up an outreach centre in Mexico with a budget of $1,200! When

I think back on it now, it seems absolutely crazy, but we knew God was calling us to move in radical faith. I believe He loves this kind of zealous faith. We can't allow ourselves to get so sophisticated in our thinking that we miss something beautiful that God wants to do. Child-like faith is so precious to Him.

Away we went. Each of us only took one suitcase. We only had one box of kitchen supplies. We even needed to believe for a vehicle to get down there, which thankfully He provided. We drove our way down to Tijuana, Mexico, without even having a place organized to arrive at.

Upon arriving in Tijuana, we realized it was going to be much harder than we had hoped it would be to find a place to stay. There was actually a two-year waiting list for home rentals. Not only that, but places were given to nationals before foreigners. We prayed that God would open up a door for us, and we watched Him intervene. He provided a home for us to stay in. If you can believe it, we crammed about twenty-four people into this small home that only had one bathroom!

All that said, we were as happy as could be. When you live revived—where the Spirit of the Lord is continuously filling you with joy—God can ask you to do anything and it feels like an absolute pleasure. We quickly felt love growing deep within us for the people in Tijuana. We knew that God was with us and we anticipated Him blowing our minds with what He was going to do.

Considering we all had such a heart for the poor, we knew that we were going to start this outreach by giving away what we had. We kept the clothes on our backs plus one extra pair; everything else we gave away. We kept one meal of food for ourselves and gave away everything else.

This was when we began to learn what happens when you move in generosity; you experience the generosity of heaven.

As we gave away our clothes and food, the amazing thing was that it all kept multiplying and coming back to us. The more clothes we gave away, the more we would receive ourselves. The more food we gave away, the more we would receive ourselves. We discovered that when we gave to those in need, God moved in power. We would go into these extremely poor areas giving away food and clothing. Whenever we would go to an impoverished area and give of ourselves, there would be a harvest. People would get touched by the Holy Spirit.

As a team, we learned very quickly that if we want to see God move, then we need to be flexible because revival is full of surprises. When revival is present, the supernatural happens. Things will happen that we've never seen before. Things will happen that history hasn't yet recorded. We have to be ready to change our plan and to go with the flow of heaven. Jesus speaks of this when He talks about wineskins.

Mark 2:22: "And no one puts new wine into old wineskins; or else the new wine bursts the wineskins, the wine is spilled, and the wineskins are ruined. But new wine must be put into new wineskins."

Jesus says we can't put new wine into an old wineskin. The reason why, is because old wineskins are brittle and inflexible. We need a flexible wineskin to hold the new wine. If we want the new wine of revival, we can't think the way the "old man" thinks. We need to put on the "new man" and embrace what God is doing.

There would be times where we would go to a family struggling with poverty and we would move in generosity. We would come back the following day and these same people would testify of angels coming into their homes after meeting us. These people would then receive supernatural provision due to angels visiting them! They would weep in the presence of the Lord as they shared this with us, then give their lives to Jesus Christ. God was blowing our minds with how He was choosing to encounter people.

We began inviting entire families with us to come down to Tijuana. I remember one time taking a young boy with me who was only eleven years old. I brought him house to house with me throughout a very poor village, praying for the sick.

When we would see someone who needed healing, I would say to him, "Come lay hands on this person and pray for healing."

Healing would come through the hands of this little boy. It was beautiful. In every home we went to, one after another people would be healed. Every single day, we saw people healed. Every single day, we saw people saved. People were delivered of demons and filled with the Holy Spirit. God then opened up the prisons to us. We would go in and preach to the prisoners, seeing God move powerfully in jails. There was not a day that went by that the power of God didn't transform lives. Every evening during dinner, we would share testimonies from each of the groups that went out throughout the day. There were what felt like endless testimonies of people being saved, healed, and delivered all throughout Tijuana.

As we continued to move in generosity, more and more came in for us to then distribute and give away. After a while, we couldn't give everything away fast enough! There was more clothing, food, and furnishings coming in than what was going out. There was so much provision that came into our outreach centre that we actually had to get a storehouse in San Diego to hold all of the excess. We were able to furnish different ministries; we provided them with food and clothing for the poor. It was like living under an open heaven of abundance.

When we first went to Tijuana, all we had was $1,200. By the time we left three and a half years later, we had three buildings all completely furnished. We built several homes. We built an orphanage and a medical clinic. We had three vehicles. We had so much capital and material things that we were able to bless every single ministry that we partnered with. We blessed the city with everything we could. Over the years, we've stayed connected with each of these ministries and have been overjoyed watching them continue to flourish.

I learned a significant kingdom principle during this life-changing journey. The principle is this: when you sow, you will reap. *Whatever* you sow, you will reap. If you sow the gospel, you will reap souls. If you sow healing prayers, you will reap healing. If you sow in deliverance, you will reap deliverance. If you sow finances, you will reap finances. I learned way back in my mid-thirties, that when we lay ourselves down on the altar before the Lord, He can do remarkable things through us. I learned that God—plus nothing—equals everything we will ever need.

We need to learn to have complete dependency upon God. If we can accomplish something ourselves, then we can only do just that. However, when we need to rely on the intervention of God, that's when we see the supernatural. So in order to see the supernatural touch of heaven, we need to be totally dependent on God. When God tells us He wants us to do something and we begin thinking things such as: "I don't feel adequate for that. I don't feel like I've got what it takes. I don't feel like I have the resources to make that happen," this is the best place we could ever be. It's a sign that we are ready for revival, because only God can make it happen. We need to always remember that it's only possible because of His grace and intervention. This keeps us dependent upon Him.

Ephesians 1:3: "Blessed *be* the God and Father of our Lord Jesus Christ, who has blessed us with every spiritual blessing in the heavenly *places* in Christ."

God wants us to partake of the abundance of heaven. He doesn't want us to only experience it when we pass into eternity; He wants us to enjoy it *now*. Not only does He want us to experience it now, but He wants us to experience it for the rest of our lives. I love sharing stories of God's supernatural provision. I love testimonies of healing and deliverance; however, He doesn't want us to experience these things short-term. He wants us to live out longevity in revival. This is why if I were to speak to those who are coming after me—to those hungry for more of God—I would talk to them about Christ-like character.

I believe that God is tremendously passionate about us having Christ-like character. All throughout scripture, we can see the good, the bad, and the ugly. We can plainly see the triumphs as well as the shortcomings of different men and women; it's all recorded there. I have observed over the years people who are incredibly gifted. I've seen them live in revival for a season, but then falter because they didn't watch over their heart with all diligence. This resulted in them only running for a time, instead of finishing their race that was set before them. Unfortunately, I've seen it not only hurt themselves, but also hurt their families. I've seen it hurt the church. I've seen it hurt the lost. I've seen people end up confused because of leaders and revivalists who didn't cultivate their character. It's heartbreaking to watch. It's heartbreaking to see a disqualification.

Even in scripture, God doesn't shy away from revealing these types of shortcomings. Throughout the Bible He exposes those who were evil in heart. Even though some were anointed by Him, they still decided to do evil in the sight of the Lord. Over the years, we have witnessed people of great gifting and anointing being powerfully used by God in revival and harvest, go on to have very public falls. Unfortunately, this is the by-product of not watching over our heart and character. It's important to know that we are remembered for how we present the Lord. Not only that, but this is what determines our longevity.

Those who I love to see are the ones like Billy Graham. Billy Graham immeasurably advanced God's kingdom, while still remaining faithful to his calling all his days. Even unsaved people respect him. I believe the reason why is because he was consistent in character. These people may not have believed in Jesus, but they saw a man who was unswayable in his integrity. This is how each of us should aspire to be remembered.

Gifting is very important. Faith for the supernatural is very important. We can groom our gifting by being in the presence of the Lord, by praying, and seeking after His greater glory. It's important for us to do this because it gives us greater ability to bless God's people. As our gifting is developing, we need to foster our character. When I'm talking to people about how to groom their character, I will often say, "Never forget who you are." We need to remember that the nature of Jesus is inside of us—not just His anointing—but His nature and character. We need to allow that to be predominant.

The Bible is clear about what the deeds of the flesh are. Galatians 5:19-21 says, "Now the works of the flesh are evident, which are: adultery, fornication, uncleanness, lewdness, idolatry, sorcery, hatred, contentions, jealousies, outbursts of wrath, selfish ambitions, dissensions, heresies, envy, murders, drunkenness, revelries, and the like; of which I tell you beforehand, just as I also told *you* in time past, that those who practice such things will not inherit the kingdom of God."

When we look at all of these deeds, we should think to ourselves, "That's not who I am. That's not who God has made me to be." When we receive Jesus as our Saviour, He gives us a brand-new nature. Old things have passed away, and all things have been made new. If we see ourselves choosing an attribute of the flesh, that's when we need to come back and remember who we are.

Not only do we need to remind ourselves of who we are, but we need to also invite others to remind us who we are. One of the things that has helped me a lot is having a very good accountability team. I think it's wise to have layers of accountability. I don't want to have an accountability team just to be able to write on my website that I have one; that would be futile. I've said to my team that I work with, "If at any time you feel concerned that I am manifesting things other than the nature of Christ, nail me on it!"

In giving them this invitation, I truly mean it. I don't want to manifest the flesh. I don't want to manifest a sinful nature, because Jesus has delivered me from it. I want to remember who I am. I want to remember that I was created to love; that I was created for truth, righteousness, and justice. I was created for longevity in revival.

Whoever you are reading this right now, remember that God has amazing plans for your life. He wants you to dwell under the open heaven of revival. He doesn't want you to only live it out for a moment, but for the rest of your days. Keep guarding your heart with all diligence. Holy Spirit wants to usher revival through you; He wants the kingdom to unfold around you. He wants to invite you on a supernatural journey with Him where He will blow your mind with His goodness and His glory. He has created you to see people healed, saved, and delivered; that signs, wonders, and miracles would follow you. God wants you to experience the abundance of heaven in your life.

This is what you were created for; this is who you are.

— *Patricia King*

SHAWN BOLZ

Shawn is a TV host, as well as an author, a producer, and a Christian minister. He has been leading conversations in the church, the entertainment industry, and in social justice that have helped believers connect their faith to culture in a transformative way. Shawn's speaking, media hosting, and coaching through his unique expert perspective has brought him around the world to meet with churches, CEOs, entertainers, and world leaders. His areas of passion include: developing Christianity that brings transformation, the intersection of Christianity and popular culture, business from a faith perspective, social justice through faith, and hearing God's voice with a focus on restoring dignity to biblical-based prophetic ministry. He is the author of several bestselling books including "Translating God," "Keys to Heaven's Economy," "Breakthrough: Prophecies, Prayers & Declarations," and "Through the Eyes of Love." Shawn is also a contributing journalist online to CBN News Network, Charisma News Network along with Faith-links online.

"When Jesus came to the earth, He came with a revelation of the kingdom of God to restore all things. He came to set the world right again. I want to start conversations so we can see change brought to arenas such as politics, the arts and entertainment, and social justice."

— Shawn Bolz

Cultural Reformation
By: Shawn Bolz

Being a second-generation Christian, my parents love the church. Growing up, I remember them always being at conferences, services, events, and homegroups. I love these things as well, but ever since I was young, I've always had something that has burned deeply within me: a desire to see what God can do outside of the church. I've had a longing to see what God could do outside of programs, services, and religious duty. For as long as I can remember, I've known the importance of revival. It is an important value of mine; but I also believe the word *revival* is much broader than we realize. We are living in a time where God is raising up a wave of revivalists. However, not only those who will burn for the Lord within the four walls of the church; He is raising up those who will influence society and those who will build the culture of heaven in their spheres of influence. He is raising up sons and daughters of God who will shape history.

My first experience of what I would consider *revival activity* happened when I was in high school. Growing up, I was a part of a youth group. Many of us attended public school, but there was a group of us who were really going after the things of God. Our hearts burned for our schools, peers, and teachers. At the time, there was a woman who was a mentor to our youth leadership. Seeing our passion, she said to us, "Why don't we try something? Let's ask God where the harvest is. Let's ask Him where people will get saved—where people can be impacted by our love and our gifts."

As a group, we asked God. All of us were led in different directions. One girl ended up working in a group home for teen pregnancy crisis. As for myself, I ended up taking a job at a group home for bipolar boys that summer. Between the two of us, we adopted the heart of God for these kids. We prayed that He would move in these spheres where He had called us.

After a time of us working in these group homes, we heard there was a concert taking place featuring a famous Christian band. Both of us felt like this was an opportunity to see God impact these youth. We invited them all out. At the end of the concert there was an altar call. All of these kids who we had brought out came up to the front, giving their hearts to Jesus. Not only did they get saved, but they were so impacted that they ended up coming to our church. Word began spreading everywhere about what God did in their hearts, and it wasn't long before we had hundreds of kids in the youth group. These youth ended up bringing their parents out as well, resulting in rapid growth in our church. Many of these people, both young and old, began to get delivered from all sorts of things such as addictions, self-hatred, and mental illness.

To be honest, I think it freaked out a lot of the Christians. Many parents actually pulled their kids out of the youth group and the church because they didn't understand what was happening. That said, we knew God was moving!

We kept asking God where the harvest was, and He continued leading us to where people were eager to know Him. These people were broken, but hungry for the love of God in their lives. Sometimes I felt like our youth group was like the *Island of Misfit Toys*; but Jesus was giving these kids a place to belong. Our youth group grew drastically, and it was filled with newly saved, inner-city kids. Jesus brought us these amazing people who came from such diverse and hurting backgrounds, and we watched as He set them free and made them whole. Considering how many were getting saved, we really had to prioritize discipleship. I developed so many meaningful relationships in that season of my life.

Experiencing this ruined me in a wonderful way. I witnessed exactly what I knew God could do. I saw Jesus defy statistics of the marginalized. I saw Jesus heal, save, and deliver broken people, making them whole. Within the confines of our little church, God was showing me what His love is truly capable of. It was at this point that I wasn't content anymore with only seeing God move at church.

Shortly after graduating high school, I went to Bible College in Kansas City. I began having conversations with people and hearing about how God was breaking out in different places. The stories reminded me of what I was a part of in our youth group. Hunger was stirring within me for the kingdom, so I couldn't help myself but go to a lot of these different places to experience what God was doing. I wasn't looking for manmade hype; I was looking for places where there was genuine transformation taking place. I ended up hearing about a ministry group who had a heart to bring transformation to the culture of different regions. This group shared stories about how when Christianity was introduced to these places, it would completely change culture and society. When I heard these testimonies, my spirit blazed within me. I knew I needed to be a part of this.

Joining this ministry, we weren't only believing for God to impact individual lives, but to change the metrics of regions as well. I remember standing on the soil of a small town in Guatemala, called Almolonga. We asked God for strategy for how He wanted to impact that town. We were obedient to what we felt like God spoke. We ministered and prayed for so many people. During our time there, I can confidently say we saw a legitimate wave of revival. I remember hearing about how in Almolonga they had five jails that were all beyond capacity, but after two years of revival sweeping through, every jail was closed down. Four of the former prison buildings became youth or community centres. The fifth was left unoccupied for two full years. There was barely any crime for two years! Before we came, there was an 89% alcoholism rate, but after revival broke out for two years, it went down to 6%. We were actually seeing God transform society in the small town of Almolonga.

With this ministry we went to America, South America, Africa, and Europe, believing for God to impact regions. We would have conversations all over the world with pastors and leaders, encouraging them to believe for the people and communities around them. We would ask God together with these leaders, praying, "God, what is

Your strategy for this region? Where is our harvest field? What would it look like if You came and changed society?"

If we want to see a region impacted, we need to listen to what our culture and community are looking for. As the church, we would understand how to meet specific needs if we learned to listen to Holy Spirit and tune in to the needs of culture for specific regions. For example, it could be that there is a huge foster care surge, which might not be here five years from now—but it's here now. This would mean there is a current opportunity if we are paying attention and listening to the Lord.

Travelling and helping leaders like this by consulting with them and listening to Holy Spirit completely transformed my life. It changed the way I viewed how we can be vessels of revival. The key was this: we often talk about the absence of God's love somewhere, but we need to tap into where His love wants to invade. This is what gave us authority to bring real change. Not to bring temporal change; not only to bring more churches, but to go deeper and look at the roots of issues, which are often spiritual. Once we discern the issue, we can then ask God what His strategy is to bring about change. Sometimes the strategy was through fasting, intercession, or prayer; but that wasn't always the right key. Sometimes it was asking God for favour with the right families or members of a community. We learned to step out of a defensive posture in how we ministered. We didn't show up defeated; we showed up knowing that the love of God is powerful. It can restore even the most broken region and make it whole.

When Jesus came to the earth, He came with a revelation of the kingdom of God to restore all things. He came to set the world right again. I want to start conversations so we can see change brought to arenas such as politics, the arts and entertainment, and social justice. Otherwise, we are left with humanism or our best Christian efforts, and it's not good enough if we don't have a partnership with Holy Spirit leading it. Holy Spirit wants to lead through us.

I've had to say "no" to a lot of things I've wanted to do in order to be present with where God was in my life. When I was in my twenties, I worked in the foster care system for years. For about four years, I worked at different mental illness hospitals as a chaplain. I worked many different jobs like this to see if we could see sustainable change—and we did! It created something within me where I had a desire to be a conversationalist in how to go and engage culture.

In my twenties, a couple once contacted me who got saved out of a commune cult. They called me and asked if I could take in the grandson of the leader of this commune. There are thousands of these cults in the Midwest and the South. The leaders of these communes generally have good intentions, but they don't have good theology, practice, or accountability. These communes often turn into work labour camps where all sorts of control and abuse can manifest. Taking this boy into my home was very sobering for me. It didn't take me long to realize that he was deeply hurting. He had been separated from his parents since he was eleven years old. He lived in a group home in the campus of this cult. With his grandfather being the leader, this kid worked over ten hours per day and didn't have more than a fifth-grade education. Having this young boy with me, I found out about more boys between the ages of fifteen and nineteen who were in this similar situation. Unfortunately, their options were limited for them in foster care. No one wanted them because they had so many felonies, were going through sentencing, or had experienced so much sexual abuse. My heart broke for them. Needless to say, I decided to take some of these guys in with me.

Whether it was for two days, three weeks, or six months, I had these young men living with me. Believe me, this wasn't my "plan A" for my life in this time, but I felt like God spoke to me. He said, "Shawn, this is one of the grounds I want you to take in this season."

Making the decision to change culture often comes at a cost. We rarely talk about that, but it's true. We need to look at a situation through the eyes of heaven. This can be uncomfortable for us, but it forces us to adjust. It causes us to know God's compassion in a far deeper way. Choosing to bring in these young men wasn't about me trying to change the whole foster care system or to see every orphan healed. God showed me His perspective of what He was asking me to do. This was about how there would have been an entire crop-full of young men who would have been mistreated and mishandled if it weren't for a few of us who would rise up to walk with them. This was the harvest God had called me to.

When these boys came into my house, I felt like God said to me, "Tell them that this is a safe place and that you're going to be praying for them. Tell them that you believe in them—that no matter what they've done, you are going to love them. Let them know that if they ever want to talk about their lives, they can; if they don't want to, that's fine as well."

The first week I had three guys with me, and they would hide food under their beds because they were used to not getting enough food in their previous foster homes. These guys worked out all the time, so they were huge! That said, because of what they had endured throughout life, they were very private and very scared. At the time they had very poor social skills because they had lived their entire lives just needing to survive.

Even with all they had gone through, these were incredible young men. I would watch them over time as they would go through this process of transformation. It was all based on the revelation of, "There's a Father in heaven who loves you." All I did was provide a space of love and belief where they were given permission to dream past their current circumstances. This enabled them to begin stepping into personal freedom. When these men first came to me their only dream was to survive and hopefully live to the age of twenty-five. By the end, they dreamed of being fathers. They dreamed of helping others. As a result of what God did in their hearts, many became advocates to bring change to the foster care system in our state. By the time I moved away from Kansas, there were four boys who were getting their social welfare degrees and changing social welfare as we know it! How could this not ruin us in the best of ways?

This inspired me to start dreaming. What would it look like if we built some campuses in Africa? What if we could change some of the poorest areas of South America or Africa? With my best friend, we started up bases throughout the world, many of which are still running. This has been such a powerful tool to introduce people to the gospel and to dream beyond their hurdles in life—to hope again. We started these campuses to launch kids who didn't belong anywhere else. Our motto was, "Today you are an orphan, tomorrow you are a leader in your nation."

We've had tons of kids go through who are now leaders in their nations. They want to bring reformation and change. It's amazing to watch that this works. The kingdom works! I've witnessed it firsthand. I've seen Jesus take people everyone else had written off, yet He fashioned them into significant leaders. I've seen how personal transformation gives people hope for their region, city, or industry.

In my experience, revival is when the kingdom of heaven breaks forth and things that were God's original plan for the earth get restored. Revival isn't just when people get saved—although that's a part of it. Revival isn't only when a church grows to over one thousand people, although that can be revival activity. Revival in its purest form is when you have patterns and systems in society and you can measure the change due to God's presence intervening.

A lot of us get away from this way of thinking because of hyper-dominion theology, which believes that everything physical will belong to Jesus before He returns. This scares people from seeing any form of healthy dominion theology. We need to understand that there are areas like where Joseph, Esther, and Daniel occupied— there are places we are called to occupy to help bring about the best-case scenario. A lot of people don't say something is revival because it doesn't look the way they think it should. It might not look like revival we see in conferences or meetings. Sometimes in order for us to see revival, we need to look at the change that people need around us.

At one point in my life, I remember spending time with a specific house of prayer. They had been diligently praying for ten years, but were talking about how they hadn't seen the change they had expected in their church from their prayers. They were getting so frustrated because they were praying big prayers, but nothing was really happening. They began asking themselves questions, such as, "Are we actually accomplishing anything?" This is honestly a very good question to ask. It's important that we ask ourselves these tough questions.

During this time, I remembered watching a movie called *Bruce Almighty*. In the film, the main character, who is played by Jim Carrey, becomes God over his city. This happens because he thinks he can do a better job than God, who is played by Morgan Freeman. At one point, Morgan Freeman says, "Since you're God now, you need to answer all of the prayers that people are praying." Jim tries to figure out how he can listen to all of these prayers for a city. Finally, he decides to get everyone's prayers to come to him in the form of emails. The prayers were flooding in non-stop. Millions were pouring in. Many of them were material requests; everything from people wanting to win the lottery, to wanting a new car. However, if you pause the screen, you can see some of the other prayers. What many don't know, is that the creators of this movie wanted to find real prayers that the average person would pray. What would true heartfelt prayers be? A lot of these prayers were questions such as, "Am I going to have food tomorrow? Am I going to lose my job? Is my business going to go bankrupt? Is my dad ever going to come home?"

I remember seeing this in the movie and it moved me. The prayers that people actually pray compared to the prayers that are prayed in prayer rooms are actually completely fractured from each other. When we think of the different needs and burdens that impact people, we might think of major cultural issues such as racism, child welfare, environmental issues, finances, or political issues. However, if we look at most prayer rooms in churches, these things are marginalized to be prayed about only 1% of the time. The rest of the things we pray into are often religious agenda. In my opinion, we should be looking at specific needs that our community has. We should be looking at the different things that need to be happening in culture around us and asking God what part we play in bringing change. This can then be brought into prayer. This can be brought into action. Once we pray into these needs and act on them, then we can celebrate the small and grand victories with God. We can track our growth and breakthrough. This is how we can partner with Holy Spirit.

When I watched this movie, I said to God, "I want to know what prayers You are listening to when You are seated on the throne. I want to know what *You* are praying and interceding about." I did this because I think there can be a distinct disconnect between what we are praying for as Christians and what the actual needs of people are. This is an awesome and dangerous way to pray. I say that, because I quickly found myself caring about things I didn't give much thought to before. I found myself meditating on cultural issues that I had no idea burned within the heart of God. I began caring about becoming a voice for issues that felt very foreign and abstract to me.

A sphere where God has given me a voice to bring change and to meet the needs of people is in the arts and entertainment industry. It's amazing to see how God uses the arts to change hearts. He uses it to change society and meet needs crying out from people that we don't even realize are there.

We can look at the film *The Ten Commandments* for instance, which is one of the most viewed films in history. This film was released in 1956 during a time when humanity had a distinct need to understand what a healthy moral compass was. All of a sudden, this film came out with Charlton Heston. It completely changed people's religious views of God because they had never seen what the Bible actually looked like and how it can affect them in real life. It brought about a spiritual consciousness to who God is in one opening weekend. We can fast forward to when Mel Gibson made *The Passion of the Christ* in 2004. Over seven hundred million people have seen that movie—almost one billion people. Muslims and Buddhists saw it. These are people who would likely never set foot in a church. They were curious about Jesus and went to watch the movie, seeing the most brutal part of His life; His death for us. It stirred a staggering amount of conversation amongst people from all religions and backgrounds about Jesus and Christianity.

When you show someone in our present-day lifestyle a television show like *Little House on the Prairie,* which is one of the top television series in history, it does something to them. When you show a hurting family what a healthy family should look like, it impacts them. It trains people to be a part of a family if they don't know how to be in one. I have friends who are very passionate about adoption and they had adopted a young boy from Haiti. They would have him watch *Little House on the Prairie* because he didn't come from a functional family. This little boy was learning how to have a dad. He was learning how to have a mom. God used this show to teach him what it looks like to be a part of a family. This is amazing to me, because there wasn't one sermon series that could have done this for him. He needed a visual picture of what it looks like for him to understand how to be a son in a family.

Not too long ago, Justin Bieber used social media to begin vocalizing why he doesn't agree with abortion. Through one of his posts alone, approximately forty thousand people changed their mind about abortion, in one hour. Teenage girls who were going to give their baby up through abortion, decided not to. Lives were literally saved. Millions were influenced by his social media series about abortion. The crazy thing is, that if you got every church in North America to post the same thing—since they aren't a part of the everyday world and don't have as much influence, it would likely only have one tenth of the impact! One celebrity shared his experience of why he is anti-abortion and it literally changed culture.

I think the church has done a great job of occupying our space, but we haven't always done a great job of influencing the culture around us. I think that we have in many ways advocated for the submission of our creativity. Pat Boone was one of the early fathers of the entertainment industry. He did amazing things in film and television as an "A-list" celebrity for over thirty years. He was so big, that there were times when the Beach Boys and Elvis opened for him. This man is like a spiritual grandfather to me. He had a television show that was the top-viewed program for many years. It was wholesome television. Unfortunately, he was persecuted for the majority of his career by religious Christians. The world loved him, but the church judged his creativity.

These people who persecuted him were great people in the church; but they would say things to him like, "What you're doing has no real value."

There is dualism in the church where we say we want to reach the world, but if what we do isn't inherently spiritual, we think it's not relevant. I believe we are in a time where God is correcting us. When we look at great past revivals—whether it's Azusa Street, the Jesus People Movement, or Angelus Temple—we see a pattern where they went beyond the mandate to build church. They went into the world. Over eight million people were saved through the Jesus People Movement. A significant part of this movement was due to the music and creativity that went along with it. We had people who had boldness not only to be figures in the church, but also to be cultural figures. They had influence not just inside, but also outside.

Not too long ago, we felt to hold an event bringing together those who are doing things in the entertainment industry and missions. We did it in Hollywood with around five thousand Christians who are involved in impacting this industry. We hosted a twelve-hour assembly. We spent time honouring those who had already been making an impact, and then prayed for the future generation that God was going to raise up. We had an incredibly profound moment together. There was such a large group of people who attended who felt so alone because the church doesn't always value this type of ministry. People who had felt alone for years, had people standing with them for the first time believing with them. A lot of people came feeling overlooked, but left with more ambition and drive to do what God had asked them to do. Since then we've done many things to help people feel supported and championed in their calling to bring change in the arts and entertainment industry.

2 Chronicles 9:5-8: "Then she (the queen of Sheba) said to the king (Solomon): '*It was* a true report which I heard in my own land about your words and your wisdom. However I did not believe their words until I came and saw with my own eyes; and indeed the half of the greatness of your wisdom was not told me. You exceed the fame of which I heard. Happy *are* your men and happy *are* these your servants, who stand continually before you and hear your wisdom! Blessed be the Lord your God, who delighted in you, setting you on His throne *to be* king for the Lord your God! Because your God has loved Israel, to establish them forever, therefore He made you king over them, to do justice and righteousness.'"

A part that I love in this verse, is when the queen of Sheba says to Solomon, "Your God has loved Israel, to establish them forever, therefore He made you king over them…" This is the heart of God. God doesn't necessarily gift us for our sake; He gifts us because He loves those around us. He wants to give us influence, so we can change culture for those around us.

There is so much self-criticism in the church. I mean that in the sense that if we have an idea of what to do, someone else might come against it and tear it down. There's a hierarchy within the church that is self-destructive. It's not healthy and it's not a display of humility. I think a lot of the time we forget what Jesus' first message was. Take a look at this:

Matthew 5:14-16: "You are the light of the world. A city that is set on a hill cannot be hidden. Nor do they light a lamp and put it under a basket, but on a lampstand, and it gives light to all *who are* in the house. Let your light so shine before men, that they may see your good works and glorify your Father in heaven."

No one lights a lamp and puts in under a bowl. God wants to give you the greatest place where you can shine from. We actually stifle a lot of ambition to change the world by trying to keep people small; by trying to snuff out their light. It's important that we see God move in these areas that the church doesn't have direct control over. Unfortunately, when we move in creativity, we will often be more persecuted by Christians than by the world. Therefore, we need to see what God is doing outside the walls of the church, so that when religion comes against us, we can stand on our testimony of what we've seen God do. When this happens, we are able to stand on solid ground—able to say, "My God has placed me here."

Whoever you are reading this book, you need to know that God wants to give you a platform to shine from. Don't be ashamed of it. Stick around conversations that are a part of change. Don't go in circles having conversations about what's not happening; focus on what God is doing in you and through others. This will keep you grounded. This will keep you passionate. This will help you remember who God is and who He has created you to be.

God wants to raise you up to influence culture. He wants to use you to shape history. Don't hide your light; shine from the platform God has called you to stand upon.

— *Shawn Bolz*

STACEY CAMPBELL

Stacey Campbell is a prophetic voice to this generation and has a passion to teach believers to know how to hear the voice of God through proper teaching and strong values. She is the founder of the Canadian Prophetic Council, and has helped launch prophetic roundtables in several nations. She serves as an honorary member of the Apostolic Council of Prophetic Elders, presided over by Dr. Cindy Jacobs. Stacey and her husband, Wesley, are founders of a mercy organization for children at risk, called "Be A Hero." Stacey is a board member of Iris Global and together she and Wesley serve on the Apostolic Team of HIM (Harvest International Ministries). In addition, they are the authors of five books and the "Praying the Bible" CD series. They have ministered in over seventy nations, labouring to see people, cities, and nations transformed. The Campbells have five grown children and live in Santa Maria, California, where they are part of the Healing Rooms of the Santa Maria Valley.

"A prominent part of keeping our heart with all diligence is to keep oil in your lamp at all times. We can't allow ourselves to run dry. We need to be receiving from Him continually."

— *Stacey Campbell*

Marked by Revival
By: Stacey Campbell

It amazes me how the Lord chooses to mark us. He ignites a flame within us, not with the wisdom of this world; but with the wisdom of heaven. He marks us through encounter.

God sparked a fire within me for personal revival when I was a child—about six years old. It was during a vacation Bible school in Beechy, Saskatchewan. One of the teachers at the Bible school showed us a flannelgraph with pictures of Jesus appearing to all the little kids. He would invite them onto His lap, saying, "Let the little children come to me." Even though flannelgraphs were a simple tool of their time to communicate the Bible, I remember being greatly impacted by this.

Later that evening, I was with my twin sister. We were raised in a traditional home, so it was customary for us to get down on our knees beside our bed to pray before going to sleep. That night when I got down on my knees, I said to God, "Lord I would love to see you like those little kids saw you." I was childlike in my prayer, but it was enough to move God.

That night I had an encounter. I can't tell you whether I was awake or asleep. I couldn't tell you if it was a dream or a vision; but it was one of the most gripping encounters of my life. In this encounter, Jesus came to me. When He appeared, He didn't look like the Jesus who I saw on the flannelgraph. In this encounter He was great in size. Since I knew it was Jesus, I began running towards Him; however, as I ran, He began to speak. At the sound of His voice, I could no longer run. I immediately fell to my knees, covering my head with my hands. His voice boomed like thunder, yet at the same time sounded like many waters. I didn't only hear his voice on the outside of me; I heard it inside of me. It filled every fibre of my being.

He said, "Christ has died!" His voice was like the shout of an avalanche.

"Christ has risen!" It was like a clap of waves.

The loudest of all, He said, "Christ will come again!"

That experience transformed my life forever. I knew beyond any shadow of a doubt that Jesus is real, that He died and rose; that He is coming again. It wasn't just hearing about Jesus that moved me in such a profound way. It was an encounter. Both biblically and historically, we can see that personal revival begins in the place of encounter. Take a look at this:

Acts 9:3-6: "As he (Saul) journeyed he came near Damascus, and suddenly a light shone around him from heaven. Then he fell to the ground, and heard a voice saying to him, 'Saul, Saul, why are you persecuting Me?' And he said, 'Who are You, Lord?' Then the Lord said, 'I am Jesus, whom you are persecuting. It *is* hard for you to kick against the goads.' So he, trembling and astonished, said, 'Lord, what do You want me to do?' Then the Lord *said* to him, 'Arise and go into the city, and you will be told what you must do.'"

It was an encounter with God that gave Paul a true revelation of who Jesus was. It was an encounter with God that transformed Saul to become Paul. It transformed him from being a persecutor of the church, to an apostle. If we want revival, this is what we need: a life-changing encounter with Him.

After encountering the Lord as a young child, from that moment on I knew instinctively that He wanted me to do good and not evil. I believe it was through this encounter that I truly became prophetic. I didn't only hear God's voice; His voice filled me. As a child, I had the Spirit of the fear of the Lord (Isaiah 11:2). I knew in that moment what was right and what was wrong; what is good and what is evil. This resulted in me becoming the white sheep in my family. I always knew when something was going on that wasn't right.

When we talk about personal revival, we need to understand that the gift of the Spirit of the fear of the Lord is precious. What we don't understand is that revival often takes people out because they don't have the fear of the Lord. They don't follow through in their pursuit of God because they have gifts without the Spirit of the fear of the Lord.

Proverbs 1:7: "The fear of the Lord *is* the beginning of knowledge, *but* fools despise wisdom and instruction."

Proverbs 8:13: "The fear of the Lord *is* to hate evil."

A key to understanding the Spirit of the fear of the Lord is found in Proverbs 4:23, which says, "Keep your heart with all diligence, for out of it spring the issues of life." A prominent part of keeping our heart with all diligence is to keep oil in your lamp at all times. We can't allow ourselves to run dry. We need to be receiving from Him continually. We need to allow Him to keep our heart healthy in Him; this is what the Spirit of the fear of the Lord does. Take a look at this story:

Luke 8:43-48: "Now a woman, having a flow of blood for twelve years, who had spent all her livelihood on physicians and could not be healed by any, came from behind and touched the border of His garment. And immediately her flow of blood stopped. And Jesus said, 'Who touched Me?' When all denied it, Peter and those with him said, 'Master, the multitudes throng and press You, and You say, 'Who touched Me?' But Jesus said, 'Somebody touched Me, for I perceived power going out from Me.'"

When Jesus went into the crowd and the woman with the issue of blood touched him, He literally felt power and virtue leave Him. If you read about the old revivals, they would often talk about how they would get so tired. I don't believe this was necessarily due to a lack of sleep. It's that when people are putting a draw on the Spirit—a draw on the anointing—it also puts a draw on us. The anointing no doubt comes from God, but we are the vessel. If we are not before God by ourselves filling up every day, then there will be more output than input. I believe this is why the principle of Sabbath is one of the Ten Commandments. We need to actually keep enough oil in our own lamp. There can be a unique demand that comes with revival. If we aren't guarding our heart, this demand can easily make us lose our own personal relationship with God. The success of it can keep you running every day of the week with no breaks. We need to remember to rest in the Lord. It's in this place that we are filled. It's in this place where we keep our heart with diligence.

There are two great tests of wealth: the test of abundance and the test of lack. I believe the test of abundance is greater than the test of lack. I believe we experience this in revival when we are experiencing the blessings of abundance. Whereas lack puts us in a position where we are crying out to God, the test of abundance asks us if we will continue to cry out once we've stepped into promise. Many people stop pushing for Him once they've stepped into the abundance of heaven. Lack puts us in a position of depending upon God. However, when we can have anything we want in the spirit realm such as healings, miracles, wealth, fame, or whatever else comes, we need to keep our heart in check. This is why the test of abundance takes more people out than lack does.

I've also noticed that people think they are indispensable because they see themselves as God's "man or woman of the hour with the power." Pride can come in. This is why the Spirit of the fear of the Lord is so important. If we are not before God, seeking Him and leaning not on our own understanding, what happens is we think that the power is us. We forget that we are completely dependent on it coming from God and our relationship with Him. Even though the gifts are irrevocable, we can end up with a gift without relationship. The gift might still work, but you can't even tell that you've lost your relationship with God Himself. If this occurs, all we have is a gift with no presence. You can always tell when people are ministering from the presence, compared to just gifting. There is a clear distinction.

I've found that the fear of the Lord can at times be quite painful, because things that may be obvious to me aren't always obvious to others. This is why I've learned that the fear of the Lord needs to be partnered with a revelation of mercy. I feel that when I was younger, my understanding of the fear of the Lord made me less merciful and more critical; even judgmental at times. I would say things like, "People should just be better." The problem was that I understood holiness without mercy. Fortunately, I'm married to a man whose primary gift is mercy. It's a good balance for me. The fear of the Lord needs to be paired with a revelation of mercy.

Many years ago I had an experience concerning this where the Lord humbled and impacted me quite profoundly. This occurred when I was in university. At the time, I was always attending church multiple nights per week. Being Plymouth Brethren, I was very conservative, but I loved God. I wanted to be anywhere where I could know Him more.

One night, I went to a Christian barbeque. At one point during the event, I went into the washroom and saw a woman throwing up into the toilet. I didn't have words for it back then, but when I witnessed this it felt like something jumped onto me. Even though I was having encounters with God and experiencing the spirit realm, I didn't have language to understand something so blatantly spiritual.

As I watched the woman throwing up, it was as though I heard a voice in my head, saying, "That's a good idea, you should do that." Due to what I had experienced that evening, I developed an eating disorder overnight.

I know now that this was the enemy, but at the time I didn't understand what was happening. The next time I ate, I forced myself to throw up afterwards. I would go through stints where for three weeks at a time, I was so severely bulimic that I was throwing up three to five times per day. There were other times when I wouldn't eat for three weeks straight. It was horrible. I experienced this consistently for eight solid months. I was already a Christian, yet I was experiencing this torment. I was in my third year of university studying French and German. I was in my first year of marriage. My husband, Wesley, was going through Bible college. He was studying the Bible every day, yet I was experiencing this secret sin that I knew was wrong, but I didn't know how to fix it. I didn't even want to tell anyone because I was always able to be good. I had the Spirit of the fear of the Lord, which empowered me to always do the right thing, but I battled so much shame. I was out of control and I couldn't control my own eating. I was praying every day—reading my Bible every day. I would read verses about the love of God, but I wouldn't feel good enough or deserving of it because I was battling this issue.

In this time, when I did eventually tell people, there wasn't a lot of understanding around eating disorders. There weren't the same tools and resources that there are today. Therefore, I would share my struggle, but no one had context for what I was battling. No one knew how to help me. I quickly realized I had no strength on my own to fight this. It wasn't about my own righteousness. It wasn't about my own goodness. In fact, I was a full-blown addict to food and I couldn't save myself.

One day, I was attending a service at a Mennonite Brethren church. Worship was taking place and the worship leader was singing about the love of God. I was at the point where I didn't even know if God liked me because I wasn't good; because I had my own personal struggle. It was at this moment that I saw a vision.

I was wide awake, and I saw it just as clearly as you and I would be able to see one another. I saw a bright light over the head of the worship leader. I could see it with my eyes open and I could see it with my eyes closed. I saw Jesus. He had His arms open, stretched out wide to me. It felt like wave after wave of liquid love was washing over and through me. This wasn't an intellectual thing I could understand with my mind; it was tangible. I could feel it in the very core of my being. For about fifteen minutes of experiencing this, I wept and cried.

I then heard an audible voice, saying, "Even if you struggle with this until the day you die, I will still love you."

This was the moment I was healed from my eating disorder. I understood that it isn't by works that we are saved, lest anyone should boast. I began to understand holiness and mercy. I understood that mercy didn't diminish holiness. This encounter solidified within me a grace for myself and for others. I understood that the fear of the Lord needs to be paired with a revelation of mercy.

My husband is fifth generation Plymouth Brethren. This renewal movement was founded back in the early 1800s. It was a movement to get back to the Bible. We would sing a cappella with no instruments. We would share words if we had a word; however, women weren't allowed to speak in church. As women, we wore head coverings in the church and I was always silent. It was very conservative. The founder of this movement was very influential in the doctrine of Cessationism. He would teach things such as how we hear a lot about healings and miracles in the book of Acts, but by the time we get to the epistles, we hardly hear about it anymore. He was very instrumental in bringing a doctrine where it is believed that all of the gifts of the Spirit ceased to exist after the church of Acts. Therefore, anything that existed after-the-fact was demonic. All that said, we were completely against the whole idea of manifestations of the Holy Spirit and the gifts of the Spirit. I would argue with people who believed in the gifts of the Spirit to try to convince them otherwise. Since the Plymouth Brethren loved the Word of God, I knew the Bible quite well, so I was able to make what I considered at the time to be a strong case. In Bible college, my husband even wrote a paper entitled, "Why Tongues are Not for Today." Everything we came by with the Holy Spirit, we weren't in pursuit of initially. We weren't eagerly desiring the gifts of the Spirit. We simply didn't believe in it.

Even though we didn't understand the function of the Holy Spirit, we were always hungry for God. We loved Him. One of Wesley's teachers in his fourth year of Bible college had been to a John Wimber class in seminary. John would come in and give lectures on signs and wonders in that particular class. Wesley was so zealous with questions, so when the teacher said that John Wimber was going to be ministering in Vancouver, he suggested we go hear him. At the time, we had planted a very conservative Baptist church, so this was way out there for us. Wesley really wanted to go, but I was much more skeptical. He is generally more outgoing in his personality than I am. I was much more analytical.

Wesley and our friend David Ruse went together to this particular conference featuring John Wimber. The conference had about twenty-five hundred people attending. Wesley went to all the courses available, and he would come home completely jazzed by what he was experiencing. I remember him saying to me, "Stacey, I knew there had to have been something more! I knew that we could still see miracles... I just knew it!"

At the time, I had been steeped in the Cessationalist teachings for years, so I was still skeptical and didn't go to the courses. However, one time I went to go pick him up and I ended up arriving at ministry time. It was shocking to me!

When I walked into the church, John Wimber said, "Come Holy Spirit."

There were people all the way up in the balcony laughing uncontrollably in the Spirit. It was a bit nerve-wracking walking in and seeing all these people laughing so undignified. I remember thinking, "I need to get out of here. These people are so emotional..."

When I came closer to the centre of the sanctuary, I saw people kneeling on the ground weeping. Tears streamed down their faces. The most alarming thing to me—I will never forget it—was a man standing in the centre aisle screaming and bending down, over and over again. He screamed so loudly. I remember looking up at John Wimber who stood up on the stage. He put his reading glasses on, resting them upon the crook of his nose. He was looking at the guy screaming and said, "Oh don't worry about that. That's just rage."

I thought, "That's rage?"

I didn't understand this. People were laughing, weeping, and in rage… I thought to myself, "These people are demon possessed at best and mentally deranged at worst! They are so emotional!"

Afterwards, I said to my husband, "Wesley, this can't be God…"

He said, "Stacey, you won't believe it. I need to show you…" He showed me line by line in scripture about how everything was completely biblical.

I replied saying, "That will never happen to me, because I'm not emotional."

To say I was wrong would be a dire understatement.

During the period of us planting our Baptist church, there was a worship event taking place with the Vineyard. David Ruse ended up going and had a powerful encounter with the Holy Spirit at this conference. He was the first person I had personally met who got hit by the Spirit in this way. This time I knew it was real because I knew he wasn't crazy! Suddenly, there was a newfound hunger for prayer in our leadership meetings. One particular night, we invited some prophetic people we had heard of to come to our church. As these people were praying in this small room for someone else, the Spirit of God began to fill me from my toes, up to the top of my head. They weren't even praying for me! My feet began shaking, and then my legs. I was so embarrassed, so I tried to stop but I couldn't. My body began bouncing off the chair. Then my head began shaking. With no one even praying for me, I began speaking in tongues. It came out from my innermost being. It was like a river coming out. Like a wind. I spoke in tongues at the top of my lungs. There was no one more shocked than me.

These things began to trickle from person to person in our small Baptist church. People didn't know what was going on, including Wesley and me. One night at a Christmas party with all the elders and all the leaders, the Spirit of God fell like in Acts 2. Out of nowhere, three of us in a room of about twenty were filled with the Holy Spirit and began to prophesy. I had never prophesied before. God began to speak to us. I was prophesying about things that were going to happen in the future about different nations. I said things I didn't know before. I prophesied about the upcoming generations. For hours, we prophesied. We didn't have a single charismatic in the group; we were Plymouth Brethren!

The Spirit of God moved like a wildfire after that. People would just walk into our church and it was like an atmospheric revival. People who weren't even saved would just begin crying, not knowing why. They would get saved. We would have continual baptisms, because so many people were being saved. People would literally try to jump into the hot tub to get baptized and saved. We would have up to seventy people getting baptized on a Sunday. People would fall, weep, shake, and prophesy. People would be healed. People would publicly repent of their sins. These phenomena swept throughout the church, community, and Bible college. Our little Baptist church of thirty-five people grew to be the fastest-growing Baptist church in Canada. Our church grew from zero to fifteen hundred in just a few years.

I've learned that there is a direct link between prophecy and revival. Acts 1:8 says, "You shall receive power when the Holy Spirit has come upon you; and you shall be witnesses to Me in Jerusalem, and in all Judea and Samaria, and to the end of the earth." We see here that we will receive power when the Holy Spirit comes upon us, but what is this power for? It is to become a witness. When there is power, there is revival. We know this biblically, as well as historically. We all know the story of Acts 2:1-4. When the Spirit came, they all began to look like they were drunk and began to declare the wonderful works of God in multiple languages. When Peter stands up to give a description, he quotes the prophet Joel:

Acts 2:17: "And it shall come to pass in the last days, says God, that I will pour out of My Spirit on all flesh; Your sons and your daughters shall prophesy, your young men shall see visions, your old men shall dream dreams."

The power to become a witness is a prophetic power. When prophecy hits either for the masses or for an individual, it is all about revival. Thousands can get saved in a day. Scripture commands that we eagerly desire prophecy. In 1 Corinthians 14:1 it says, "Pursue love, and desire spiritual *gifts*, but especially that you may prophesy." I believe the reason why is because there is a direct link between prophecy and salvation. There is a direct link between prophecy and revival.

Since we were having all of these experiences with our church, we weren't allowed to be Baptists anymore. Thankfully a door opened for us to join the Vineyard church. Three months before the Toronto outpouring, John Arnott invited Wesley to come speak at their family camp. At the end of each night they would spend time together.

One night, Wesley said to John, "We've been experiencing things that we can't explain." Wesley played John our prophecy tapes. He heard the spontaneous prophetic utterances as the Spirit of God would come upon us.

"Can they do that here?" John asked.

Wesley laughed, "Oh yes, they can do it anywhere."

In October of 1993, Wesley was asked to speak at a church in Barrie, Ontario. He asked me, as well as a few other prophetic voices from our church to come along so we could see John and his wife Carol. At the time, Toronto Airport Church had only been going for a few years. When we arrived, we began our prayer time with them. The Spirit of God came upon me I began manifesting under the power of God. John and Carol had never seen anything like that at the time. To be honest, I think they were a little freaked out. I began to prophesy saying, "You are a father. You are a father, John. There is coming a great move of the Holy Spirit, but the danger will be that people begin to focus on the manifestation and forget that their names are being written in the Lamb's book of life."

That was October 1993. When Randy Clark went there on January 20 in 1994, John Arnott came home from that meeting and called Wesley saying, "Wesley, it's happening! Everything that Stacey said. The Spirit has begun to fall. It's happening!"

He phoned us every night after the meeting saying we needed to get down there. Wesley was there seven times in the first year, and I went up with him three or four times. The Spirit just began to fall. I remember being at those meetings to prophesy, and when I would prophesy the Spirit would literally fall upon hundreds of people. It was absolutely crazy.

Shortly after that, John Wimber was putting on an event in Anaheim and invited four of the key couples who were a part of the Toronto Blessing to attend their conference. The sanctuary for the conference held three thousand people and they had two thousand in the overflow room. Wesley was preaching that night, and at the end he asked me to come up to the front to prophesy. At that point, I didn't prophesy much publicly, but boldness came upon me. When I got up to the stage, the Spirit of God came upon me and I began to prophesy. I was prophesying and shaking under the power of God. When I prophesied, it was like the old revival testimonies you would hear from the Cane Ridge Revival. A roar came up from the crowd that was like the roar of Niagara Falls. The Spirit of God literally filled the room. People began screaming and roaring. It was so loud that I thought an accident had happened in the pews.

At one point, I stopped prophesying and said, "What's going on? Is everything okay?"

Wesley looked at me and said, "Keep going. Keep going."

Wesley told me afterwards that as I was prophesying people were literally being lifted up and being thrown three or four rows back, shaking, and weeping in encounters with God. The power of heaven was hitting the entire room.

Once I had gotten off the stage, a pastor came up to me saying, "I need to apologize to you. When I came in here, I was very critical; but when you began to prophesy, I was thrown forward three rows and I had a vision…"

This is what happens when the prophetic is released. Revival happens. People are saved. People encounter the heart of God.

I truly believe we are living in a time where God is wanting to release a prophetic roar throughout the church. He is raising up radical lovers of Jesus who will have the sensitivity to hear His voice and the boldness to speak His word. He is raising up a people who will carry the Spirit of the fear of the Lord; those who will be moved by an encounter with His heart. He is raising up those who are rooted in friendship with Him.

In this very day, God is marking us for revival.

— Stacey Campbell

Dr. Rodney Howard-Browne

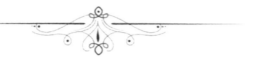

Drs. Rodney and Adonica Howard-Browne are the founders of Revival Ministries International, The River at Tampa Bay Church, River Bible Institute, River School of Worship, and River School of Government in Tampa, Florida. With a passion for souls and a passion to revive and mobilize the Body of Christ, Drs. Rodney and Adonica have conducted soul-winning efforts throughout fifty-seven nations with Good News campaigns, R.M.I. Revivals, and the Great Awakening Tours. As a result, millions of precious people have come to Christ and tens of thousands of believers have been revived and mobilized to preach the gospel of Jesus Christ.

"God hasn't made you so that you will eventually fizzle out. His purpose for your life is for revival. He wants His fire to burn in you. He wants you to finish your race. He wants you to last."

— Dr. Rodney Howard-Browne

The Fire of God
By: Dr. Rodney Howard-Browne

I received a heart for revival when I was just a child.

I was born and raised in South Africa. I grew up in the Pentecost movement, being born again and baptized in the Holy Spirit when I was eight years old. My parents used to have prayer meetings at our house where God would show up so powerfully. There were times when people would need to be carried out of the house because God's presence was so tangible. People would be delivered of devils; many were healed from physical pain and sickness. I grew up seeing major miracles that were undeniable.

My pastor at the time—who has now gone on to be with the Lord—was greatly impacted by revival in the 1950s; so he was pushing for signs, wonders, and miracles. We used to have what we would call "Wall of Jericho" services. I remember being in these services. God would move in such a way where people would be flying all over the place due to His power. I remember being so undone by God, that even as a child, I would need to be carried out of the meeting because I was lost in His presence. There was also an evangelist that we were connected with who helped pioneer about seven hundred churches across Southern Africa. This man was greatly influenced by the healing revival from the 1940s. When you put this combination of people together and they are ministering to you, it grabs a hold of you. When you grow up like this, you can't get away from it. Heaven marked me. Revival marked my life.

Even as I boy, I knew I was called to preach. I had seen many preachers who spoke at different churches. Their messages sounded good, but it was as though they were only giving information. I didn't see the power of the gospel to back up what they said. In 1 Corinthians 2:4 it says, "And my speech and my preaching *were* not with persuasive words of human wisdom, but in demonstration of the Spirit and of power."

I knew that if I was going to go into ministry, I needed to have the fire of God upon my life. I didn't want to just speak; I wanted people to be impacted by the Holy Spirit. I needed His power to back up my words. This started my quest to receive the fire of God in my life.

Throughout my teenage years, the Lord touched my life many times. There were moments when He would speak audibly to me. I had many supernatural dreams of different things that would take place. However, it was through an encounter in July of 1979 when the fire of God fell upon me. This completely transformed my life. It set me ablaze! Not only was I personally impacted by this, but it was this encounter that launched me into ministry.

In the first few years of being in ministry, I saw outbreaks of revival. I saw the power of the Holy Ghost pouring out over individuals, churches, and cities. The Lord then spoke to me saying, "As America has sown missionaries over the last two hundred years, I am going to raise up people from other nations to come to the United States of America. I am sending a mighty revival to America." In December of 1987, my wife and I with our three children moved from South Africa to the United States. We knew that we were called by God as missionaries from Africa to America.

In April of 1989, I was speaking at a church in Clifton Park, New York, on a Tuesday morning. I opened my Bible and began to read Luke 4:18-19, which says, "The Spirit of the Lord *is* upon Me, because He has anointed Me to preach the gospel to *the* poor; He has sent Me to heal the brokenhearted, to proclaim liberty to *the* captives and recovery of sight to *the* blind, *to* set at liberty those who are oppressed; to proclaim the acceptable year of the Lord."

I was about ten minutes into speaking when the whole atmosphere began to change. It felt like air particles began to move and the air became holy. People began to fall out of their seats. Some began to weep, and others were filled with great joy. I was shaking under the power of God, watching what was taking place.

It's one thing when you're finished preaching and everyone has their heads bowed to pray, and then God moves. People think that if God is going to move, then He's going to move then; but this was different. This was in the middle of my preaching. I can imagine that this is how Peter must have felt when he was preaching at Cornelius' house in Acts 10:44, which says, "While Peter was still speaking these words, the Holy Spirit fell upon all those who heard the word." I had to preach above the noise of the people. It was like standing in front of a rushing river. The Holy Spirit was having His way, moving and transforming people right before my eyes.

I immediately realized that we were going to start being persecuted for what was happening. I wasn't wrong; the critics and naysayers came. Some felt that what was happening wasn't scriptural. Others felt that the Holy Spirit was being interrupted. What they didn't realize was that the Holy Spirit was the one causing the disruption. He was moving upon people. He was ushering in the fire of God. He was waking people up.

This was the beginning of a revival of signs, wonders, and miracles. This movement still continues today. It has resulted in thousands of people being touched and changed as they encounter the presence of the living God.

In March of 1993, I came to Lakeland, California, for a camp meeting. The church that we were with wasn't doing well; in fact, it was on the brink of closing down.

I sat with the pastor, saying, "You and I preach very different things. I need to warn you to let you know that I'm not going to change my message when I speak."

The pastor looked at me, saying, "Well obviously what we've been preaching hasn't been working, so you might as well come on anyways."

I came to preach. On Monday morning, there were five hundred people in attendance. As I spoke, the fire of God fell in the meeting. Due to what happened in the morning, Monday night fifteen hundred people came out. By the end of the week, there were five thousand. By the second week, we had six thousand. By the end of the fourth week we had eight thousand. Within the first six weeks, we saw over one hundred thousand people come through the doors! God was moving, shaking, and reviving.

I've learned from experience that it isn't wise to stay in one area for too long when God moves in this way. When this happens in one particular place for an extended period of time, people can begin to worship the church or the city. That was when the Lord spoke to me.

He said, "I want to do this in many cities."

Obeying the Lord, I went to Fort Worth and the same thing happened there. We were there for six weeks as the fire of God fell, transforming lives. The supernatural fire of God fell in such a way that fire trucks came to the church because they saw literal flames on the roof of the building! We saw the same thing happen in many cities throughout 1993.

January of 1994 came, and we had over twenty-four thousand people registered for a camp meeting we had planned. I remember preaching in one of the meetings, and there was a unique anointing that came. People felt as though God was wrapping His arms around them in an embrace. Suddenly in the meeting, angels began singing audibly. It was such a heavenly sound. It sounded like it was being sung a semitone higher than what other people normally sing. Everyone was riveted by it. We've had this happen several times in our meetings.

When you experience things like this, persecution is bound to come. People have often asked me how I manage the persecution that has come against what we have experienced. I'm always reminded that we need to continue to give glory to the Lord. This means that if we get offended by the persecution, we are inadvertently trying to receive the glory for ourselves. We can't say, "Lord I give you all the glory," and then get mad because they're attacking us. Jesus said in John 14:10, "Do you not believe that I am in the Father, and the Father in Me? The words that I speak to you I do not speak on My own *authority;* but the Father who dwells in Me does the works." Jesus knew that the works He did were from the Father, so why should we think any differently?

People come up to me all the time, saying, "I don't like your meetings."

I just smile and say, "Well, I like them."

It's true; I do like them. I like them because I believe God does. He loves seeing people saved, healed, and delivered. He loves seeing people awakened, revived, and transformed.

The bottom line is that persecution will never go away. We are persecuted in our ministry far more now than we were even in the 1990s. It's horrendous, like a machine gun. However, you can't hold onto it. You can't focus on it; you need to just keep focusing on Jesus. There isn't time to give attention to the persecution, because people need a touch from God. Considering what we've seen, I know that the persecution we have experienced is well worth it. For me, I just keep saying, "God I give you all the glory." This way I can keep my heart clean from offense.

1 Corinthians 9:24-26: "Do you not know that those who run in a race all run, but one receives the prize? Run in such a way that you may obtain *it*. And everyone who competes *for the prize* is temperate in all things. Now they *do it* to obtain a perishable crown, but we *for* an imperishable *crown*. Therefore I run thus: not with uncertainty. Thus I fight: not as *one who* beats the air."

Considering all I've seen and experienced throughout decades of ministry, I often find myself thinking of the generations that God is currently raising up. I find myself thinking of those who will come after me. If I were to share a word with them, I would say this:

When we are talking about revival and stewarding the fire of God in our life, we need to remember that this is a cross-country race, not a hundred-metre dash. Over the span of my time in ministry which has lasted more than forty years, we have seen over twenty-nine million decisions for Jesus from all over the world. I thank God for every precious soul that has been saved. I thank Him for every life that has been touched. I've learned that it is very important to run hard for God, but it's also important to stop and smell the roses. So many young people are in such a hurry, which causes them to miss out. Don't allow yourself to miss out on what God has for you. When you get married, take time with your spouse. There is nothing wrong with going on a holiday. There's nothing wrong with going fishing. Don't deprive yourself of the things God has placed in your heart to enjoy. You are a human being; you don't have a glorified body yet. Therefore, if we want to have a lasting mark, then we need to understand the importance of longevity.

Make sure you live a life where you are relying on the Lord and not yourself. Allow Him to develop in your heart total reliance upon Him. Stay humble. Remain teachable. Stay in the word of God; it's the plumb line. We can't go off chasing doctrines that don't lead us anywhere. Many people are so shaky because they aren't rooted in the Bible. When you build a house, you need to use a plumb line. If you don't have a proper foundation, then you're in severe trouble. The first storm that comes will blow the house right down. We need to remain rooted in the truth of Jesus. God hasn't made you so that you will eventually fizzle out. His purpose for your life is for revival. He wants His fire to burn in you. He wants you to finish your race. He wants you to last.

Take a look at this:

When Peter went up to Jerusalem to tell the apostles what had happened at Cornelius' house, he said to them in Acts 11:15: "And as I began to speak, the Holy Spirit fell upon them, as upon us at the beginning." There's an important key for us here. Peter was there in the beginning. He was there when the Holy Spirit poured out in Acts 2 in the upper room. He didn't say that Cornelius experienced a lesser degree of what they received in the upper room. He didn't say, "We got the real outpouring, but they got something lesser." He said that they received the same thing!

This is where people go wrong. People often look back to times and places when God moved, and say, "That was a real genuine move of God, and we just got the leftovers." That's not true. In every tribe and tongue—in every generation—there are new people hungry for God. When He comes and touches them, it's like the very first time.

We need to understand that revival has never stopped. I meet many people who say, "I want to go back to the 1990s because of what God was doing then." I am so thankful for what God did in the 1990s—we saw amazing things—but I wouldn't go back there for anything in the world. You couldn't offer me enough money to get me to go back there. I want to be present in what He is doing now. In the last two years, we've gone to one hundred fifty-six cities from all over the world. We want to mobilize the church to win souls. This is what we've been doing since the beginning, and we aren't stopping. I'm not someone longing for the past, and I'm certainly not longing for the future. God is in the *now*. The Holy Ghost is in the *now*. God wants to pour out His fire *now!*

When God comes upon someone in this generation, it's the same as when He did in the upper room. We don't experience lesser compared to what Peter and the other apostles first received. We can't sit here thinking we need to wait for a specific year to see God to move. We can't sit wishing we were around during past moves of God.

In your day, in your generation, nation, and city God wants to move. There's an opportunity *now!*

— *Dr. Rodney Howard-Browne*

CHARLIE ROBINSON

Charlie Robinson is a Canadian revivalist and an international prophetic voice. He has spoken all over the world as a keynote speaker, ministering in a prophetic-teaching anointing and has a call to help bring in the end-time harvest. Charlie is a recognized prophetic voice to many leaders and nations. As a prophet, his words have been a catalyst for birthing several movements and ministries. They have also played a significant role in the emergence of influential leaders and have shifted nations. He is recognized as a father to many throughout the nations and has a heart for generations to live in a revelation of the glory of God.

"The kingdom of God isn't only real, but you can feel it. It isn't only real, but you can see it. You can taste it. You can touch it. God wants to reveal Himself and His glory wherever people are."

— Charlie Robinson

The Glory of God
By: Charlie Robinson

We are living in a time where a knowledge of the glory of God is being poured throughout the earth. He is raising up those who won't be satisfied with anything less than knowing Him; those who will be transformed in His presence. There is a stirring within the heart of God towards His children in this time. The stirring is this: the Father of glory wants to encounter us.

Exodus 33:18-19: "And he (Moses) said, 'Please, show me Your glory.' Then He (God) said, 'I will make all My goodness pass before you, and I will proclaim the name of the Lord before you.'"

In the early 1980s I was in adamant pursuit of God. He consumed my thoughts. I wasn't content with what I only saw on Sunday mornings. I would read the story about when Moses encountered God's glory; it deeply moved me. I knew there was more. Scripture told me so. What I felt in my spirit confirmed it. I threw myself into knowing Him. I did extended fasts; I found myself in prolonged times of prayer. Although I consider myself a revivalist, I didn't seek God for revival. I sought Him to know Him. I wanted to see His glory. I would read over and over again in scripture where Moses prayed, saying, "Show me your glory." Moses didn't pray, "Tell me about your glory." He wanted to see and experience it. I figured if Moses could pray for this, then so could I.

I would pray for the glory of God to manifest. Angels began showing up in my times of prayer; the presence of the Lord would enshroud me. When I would go about my day, people would get saved. I knew exactly why this was happening. I noticed that the more I began to focus on the glory of God, the more it began to linger upon me. Since I was seeking God, the spirit of revival began resting upon my life.

Psalm 27:13: "I would have lost heart, unless I had believed that I would see the goodness of the Lord in the land of the living."

When we carry the glory of God, amazing and unusual things take place. I'll share a story with you:

I remember a long time ago, there were a few of us who went out to do evangelism. We brought a youth team together and we worshipped out in the open in front of a skate park. As we worshipped, there were about twenty teens sitting around, watching us. After a while, the teens began shouting, swearing, and mocking us.

When we decided to stop playing music, I could feel compassion welling in me for these youth. I said, "I need to go talk to these kids."

Even as I approached these teens, they continued swearing and mocking us. I knew that when I reached them, I would need to do something. I would need to step out in faith somehow, knowing that in order to see God move we need to put ourselves out there. We need to give Him something to work with. That's when I had the idea that we needed to have a glory showdown.

When I reached them, I said, "Listen, we're going to have a showdown right now."

Many of the teens grumbled. Others laughed.

Cutting them off, I said, "Here's what we're going to do. I dare one of you to come here and let me pray for you. If I do, you're going to feel God."

When I said that, they immediately quieted because they were so caught off guard. I didn't know if any of them would take me up on my challenge, but I put the pressure on them to make a decision.

One teen, about sixteen years old wearing a baseball cap, stood up. He said, "Wait a minute... you're going to pray for me and I'm going to feel God?"

"That's right," I said.

He walked towards me, bringing his friend with him who was six feet, seven inches in height. The teenager was massive. These two guys stood in front of me. The one guy turned his hat around backwards and said to his big friend, "I'm going to close my eyes while he prays for me. If he tries to do anything to me that he shouldn't, I want you to take him out."

At this point I knew I definitely wasn't going to lay hands on him to pray, unless I wanted a black eye. I stood a few feet away from them, noticing how quiet they were. The pressure wasn't on me in that moment; it was on them. They were getting nervous. What would they do if they were wrong about their ideas of who they thought

God was?

I stretched out my hand, praying, "Lord, let your presence come upon him."

The power of Jesus hit him. What happened next, you cannot fake in the natural. He leaned backwards so far he looked like he was in the shape of a banana. Some of the teenagers let out gasps. A few screamed.

As he stood there, I was thinking to myself, "How in the world is he standing there like that?"

Minutes passed by as the teenager was under the power of God, not saying a word. Some of the girls watching him started whispering to each other. They were saying all sorts of things, trying to make sense of what was happening. They watched their friend who was lost in God's presence. As each minute passed, they began unravelling. The girls began to weep. All of the guys' faces were completely pale, their jaws dropped, including the big guy who stood in front of me.

I've learned that when people get freaked out by God, it's a good thing. It's good because people think they know everything. They think the world is how it is, and it will never change. Then all of a sudden when they encounter the Lord, they aren't so sure anymore. They crack open to a new way of thinking.

"He's hypnotized!" one of the girls shouted.

"He's not hypnotized. He feels Jesus," I said, reassuring her.

Suddenly the big guy brought his mouth to his friend's ear and shouted, "Snap out of it! Snap out of it!" No matter how loud he yelled, his friend wouldn't move.

After about twenty minutes, the young man finally leaned forwards, his body straightening out. His eyes popped opened. Right then, every one of the teenagers rushed over to him. Every one of them came to him with one question burning in them.

They all asked him, "Did you feel God?"

Awoken from his experience, he responded saying, "It was the most amazing thing... I don't know what happened. I felt like I fell into this great big pillow. For twenty minutes it felt like I was just lying in this heavenly pillow. It was the most amazing thing I've ever experienced in my life..."

Right as the words left his mouth, the big guy looked at me and said, "No way! There's no way this is real. If that's real, then do that to me!"

Before I could even respond, he stepped forward turning his baseball cap backwards just as his friend had.

I stood several feet away so they would know I wasn't touching him in any way. I said, "God, get this guy in Jesus' name."

Immediately, the big teenager started yelling and shaking, saying, "No way! No way!"

Right then, he turned around. As quickly as he could, he started running. He didn't just run; he ran as fast as I've ever seen anybody run. He ran, shouting, "No way!" over and over again until he completely disappeared into the town.

At this point I had more than a captive audience. Still blown away myself by what God did, I spoke to the teenagers about the love of Jesus. I preached the gospel to all of them. Many of them got saved.

This is what my wife, Shirley, and I try to do everywhere we go; we demonstrate the kingdom. This is what Jesus did. Not only did He talk about the kingdom— He didn't only teach about it—He also demonstrated it. The kingdom of God isn't only real, but you can feel it. It isn't only real, but you can see it. You can taste it. You can touch it. God wants to reveal Himself and His glory wherever people are. When people experience His glory, it gives them a desire, a hunger, a thirst, and a fire for Him. Revival is always a manifestation of the glory of God. Not only does He want to demonstrate His power, signs, and wonders; He wants to demonstrate His glory. God wants to do this not solely for individuals; true revival is when God touches whole people groups, cities, and nations.

For several years, I had helped host revival in Abbotsford, British Columbia. In January 2004, I was helping to put on a conference. In one of the morning meetings, Heidi Baker was speaking. The place was packed with two thousand people who were hungry for Jesus. Many respected leaders were with us. It was the fullest conference we had ever held. By the end of the service, the presence of God was so strong. Heidi was on the floor weeping. It was such a powerful time.

When I went to close the meeting, God spoke to me, saying, "Who will I send? And who will go for me?"

From the stage, I shared what God said. The place went crazy. People ran up to the front, to the altar. They were shouting and calling out to God, saying, "Send me! Send me!"

God spoke the same words to me again, "Who will I send? And who will go for me?" I released the word again, and more people came up to the front.

God spoke the word to me one last time, but before I could share it, He said, "I'm not talking to them, I'm talking to you." It was almost as though He was saying to me, "Who will I send? And who will go for me, Charlie?"

When He said this to me, I said three words. "I will go."

Immediately when these words left my mouth, I wanted to take them back because I realized I forgot to ask God where I would be going!

Suddenly, God showed me something in the spirit realm. On my right-hand side, I saw a fiery sword with a white-hot flame around it. I knew what the flame was: it was the blazing love of Jesus for the nations that I and people like me would never want to set foot in. I watched this sword as it went right into my chest. The love of Jesus for these nations bore right into my heart. I immediately fell to the ground. When I did, the microphone flew ten feet into the air. I instantly began to cry and scream because the love of Jesus for these nations was filling my heart.

As I was lying on the stage, Jesus spoke to me, saying, "I am going to send you to the dark nations of the world. You are going to go to Indonesia and to Malaysia."

Even though I was in this encounter, my flesh was saying, "No... I want to go to Florida and Hawaii!"

God said, "No, you said you will go. You're going to Indonesia and Malaysia. You're going to the dark nations of the earth."

While God was speaking this to me, Heidi walked over to me. She said, "Charlie, God is going to open up the dark nations of the world for you."

What I later found out was that the first nation Heidi and her husband, Rolland, visited was Indonesia.

I didn't tell anyone what God had said to me that night. I remember saying to Him, "I don't know anyone in Indonesia or Malaysia, so if you want me to go then you'll have to open the doors."

Not long after, I was in California ministering at a conference. When I had finished preaching, I was approached by a man from Singapore named Jedidiah Tham. Jedidiah is a good friend of mine now, but I didn't know him at the time.

He said to me, "Would you come to Indonesia and Malaysia?"

I knew that no one could have told him what God had told me. No one knew! It was so out of the blue.

I replied, saying what works really well in Canadian culture when you want to get out of something. I said, "I'll pray about it," and then I walked away.

Ten minutes later, Jedidiah came up to me again, saying, "What did God say?"

I was thinking, "Oh man! This guy is persistent, and God must really want me to go."

I said to Jedidiah, "Alright, I'll go."

I'll never forget the first time I ministered in Indonesia. On this trip, as I often did, I brought my son Samuel along with me. The pastor hosting us drove my son and me to the church where I was going to be speaking. The first meeting I was ministering at was with the church's prayer core. Being from Canada, our prayer teams for churches can be on the smaller side; often perhaps twenty people or so. That said, other than spending time in prayer, I hadn't taken time in preparation for this particular session, assuming I would only be sharing for a few minutes. Pulling up to the church, there were a few sparse cars in the parking lot, confirming my suspicions concerning how small the prayer core would be. What the pastor failed to tell me, was that there was actually a parking lot at the back of the church, brimming with vehicles.

Once inside the church, the pastor began leading me downstairs to what I expected would be a small, discreet, and quiet prayer group. That was, until a hum began to fill my ears.

With every stair I stepped down, the hum grew louder and louder until I began distinguishing words. Confused, I turned to the pastor. "What's that sound?" I asked.

The pastor smiled, "That sound you're hearing is the prayer core."

Turning the corner, I saw over three hundred people jam-packed in a small room. With no space for chairs, people prayed and interceded. The people cried out to God with all their hearts, tears streaming down their passion-filled faces.

The pastor turned to me again, saying, "This is the core of our prayer team, which is actually twenty-five hundred people. This team has been praying for two hours straight, preparing their hearts for what you're about to share with them."

My eyes went wide, knowing I hadn't prepared anything. My thoughts spun throughout my mind trying to find words, when Sammy leaned over to me.

"Dad, do you have anything?" he whispered.

Of course, I didn't. However, right when the words left Sammy's mouth, the pastor shouted, gaining the attention of everyone who was praying.

"Does the man of God from Canada have the word of the Lord?!" the pastor shouted.

Everyone quieted, looking to me.

Stunned, I said the first thing that popped into my head. I said, "Give me five minutes," then ducked around the corner.

Free from the eyes of others, I immediately fell to my face. In a panic, I cried out to God, saying, "God why did you bring me here? I don't have a word to share with these people. I don't know what I can teach them about prayer... They should come to Canada to teach us about prayer!"

Immediately, God spoke back to me, saying, "They know a lot about prayer, but they know very little about My glory. Share with them Isaiah 60:1."

I said, "Okay... I can start with that verse. What else should I say?"

"That's it," God replied.

Before I even rose from the ground, I heard the pastor from the other side of the wall shout out again, "Does the man of God from Canada have the word of the Lord?!"

I stood up, taking my place to stand before the people. A hush sounded amongst them, as I took a deep breath.

As confidently as I could, I said, "The Lord spoke to me. He told me to share Isaiah 60:1 with you." I began quoting the verse. "'Arise, shine; for your light has come! And the glory of the Lord is risen upon you.'"

Right as the verse escaped my lips, people began screaming. Some wept, while others jumped up and down. Some fell on their faces. The pastor fell to his hands and knees, weeping uncontrollably. I watched, stunned at seeing the powerful effect of the shortest message I'd ever preached.

After a significant amount of time had passed, the pastor finally stood up, the prayer core continuing to encounter the Lord. I asked him why people were responding so profoundly to what I shared.

With tears still staining his face, he said to me, "For the last seven years, people from our church have come here to pray for two hours before going to work. They go to work and then come back here to pray for another two hours before going home. For seven years we have been praying one thing, praying from one scripture alone. We've been praying, 'God, bring Isaiah 60:1 to our church. We want the glory of God.'"

This church received a touch of revival because they encountered the glory of God. We have seen miracle after miracle in that church in particular. This church has had a profound impact in stewarding revival for that nation. This is what started my journey in going to Indonesia. My wife and son have come with me many times. We've seen God do in that nation beyond what you could think or imagine. We've seen the powerful works of God; we've seen amazing signs, wonders, and manifestations of the glory of God.

One of my other times being at this church, after one of the meetings, the pastor of the church brought me into his office, telling me he wanted to show me something. He opened up his closet, pulling out two garment bags.

When he opened the first bag, I could smell the scent of acrid smoke filling my nostrils. From the bag, he pulled out a suit that looked like it had been in a fire. Charred holes were all throughout the suit. He then opened the second bag, the smoky smell amplifying. He pulled out a dress that was in similar condition as the suit; burnt with holes all throughout it.

"What happened to this suit and dress?" I asked.

The pastor explained to me that four years ago on Christmas Eve, four women who were religious radicals came to the church during a service. Each carried a box disguised as a Christmas present. What no one knew was that they were actually bombs.

These women put these bombs in four different places throughout the church, timed to detonate at the exact same time. As people worshipped Jesus, three of the four bombs went off resulting in a big explosion. The results were catastrophic. Four hundred chairs in the church were completely melted. One of the walls was blown out.

Holding the suit and dress in his hands, the pastor told me that the man and woman who wore them were sitting only a few feet away from one of the bombs. They both undoubtedly should have been killed, yet neither of them had even a scratch on them. The only person in this two-thousand-member church who was hurt was a woman who had a small scratch right above her ankle, not even big enough to need stitches.

The police and ambulances rushed to the church. Due to the severity of the destruction of the bombs, the police asked, "Where are your wounded and the dead?" knowing it would be impossible for anyone to be unharmed.

The very next day, the newspaper headlines read, "Miracle in the Christian Church." God's glory was proclaimed in a Muslim newspaper. Word spread like wildfire. In the span of a year that church grew from two thousand people to six thousand. Four thousand new converts who were formerly Muslim came to know Jesus! It's amazing to know that God likes to demonstrate His power in the presence of His enemy. It's amazing how God protects and pursues.

On December 3, 2004, I was speaking in Indonesia. I was in the glory of God—in His presence—and I was sharing what He was showing me. I recalled from the stage that the Lord showed me that there would be a terrible earthquake and a tsunami that would hit Indonesia soon. What I didn't know was that this word was recorded and sent out all over the place throughout Southeast Asia. People all over the nation were saying that this word was false, that it wouldn't happen.

On December 20 I was with Sammy in our hotel. I said to him, "Sammy, right after we leave Indonesia, there is going to be an earthquake and a tsunami."

Six days later on December 26, 2004, the earthquake and tsunami hit Indonesia. Almost two hundred fifty thousand people died in Southeast Asia. It was terrible.

God told me to go back and to tell the people, "You are not losing, you are winning."

I went back to Indonesia. While I was with Jedidiah, the phone rang. Upon answering it, he said, "It's for you. It's the head of the Indonesian Prayer Network." He handed me the phone.

The man who was the head of the Indonesian Prayer Network said to me, "We heard your prophetic word about the earthquake and tsunami before it took place. We didn't know if it was real, but once it actually happened, we knew God had spoken to you. We would like to meet you."

I agreed to meet with them.

He then said, "Great! We will send a driver to take you to a specific bank in downtown Jakarta. Go to the roof of the building, and we will have a helicopter pick you up."

I was thinking, "A helicopter? Who in the world are these people?"

The driver came and took me to the bank. Making my way to the roof—as I had been instructed—there was a helicopter waiting for me. Getting aboard, I quickly learned that this was no ordinary helicopter. There was a full-blown living room in the back of it!

I thought to myself, "What in the world am I doing here, and who are these people who want to meet with me?"

The helicopter took me to a private golf course. There were five men waiting for me to arrive. They began to introduce themselves to me. I was astounded to hear that the first man owns the second biggest bank in Indonesia. The second man who introduced himself owns the Jakarta International Airport. I quickly realized I had a meeting with one pastor and four billionaires. These four billionaires were the ones who ran the Indonesian Prayer Network. All of them wanted to meet with me because they were wondering how a man from Canada could prophesy accurately and specifically about things taking place in their country.

Since this time, I've met several Christian billionaires in Indonesia. All of them fast and pray. All of them love God. All of them use their wealth for the kingdom. In fact, the closest thing I've ever seen to a kingdom design is what I've seen in Indonesia because the businessmen love revival and they use their wealth for the kingdom. I've seen how God uses businessmen and prayer warriors to shape a nation. Ever since the earthquake and tsunami, people throughout Indonesia had been praying for mass salvations due to what took place. I talked with a good pastor friend of mine who has about twenty million people in his churches throughout Indonesia, and they estimated that within a year of that tsunami hitting, about one million people were saved throughout Indonesia.

I say all of that to say this: I've learned that God's light shines the brightest where there is darkness. Every one of us is called to seek God and His glory. This results in us becoming beacons where there is darkness; we become beacons wherever we are.

Isaiah 60:2: "For behold, the darkness shall cover the earth, and deep darkness the people; but the Lord will arise over you, and His glory will be seen upon you."

Habakkuk 2:14: "For the earth will be filled with the knowledge of the glory of the Lord, as the waters cover the sea."

Many people will hear stories such as mine, and think they are unattainable in their own lives. They will think stories of God's glory are for others and not themselves; however, we need to adjust how we think. We need to renew our minds in the fact that God wants us to experience His goodness.

Do you know how I got what I have with God? I followed Matthew 6:33 which says, "But seek first the kingdom of God and His righteousness, and all these things shall be added to you." As I mentioned before, back in the 1980s when I first began encountering God, I wasn't seeking after revival. I was never chasing after a ministry, because I didn't know if I was even called to ministry. I was seeking after God and His glory. I didn't have a lot of models to follow in my pursuit of Him. I didn't have people who could sit down with me and teach me about His glory. I pushed into God because I wanted Him; not because I wanted something from Him. I wanted a relationship with God like Paul had. I wanted to have what Moses had. I know that God isn't a respecter of persons. This means that if Moses could see the glory of God, then so can I.

So can you.

When we are talking about God's glory and revival, we need to remember something important. When we hear or read of what God did twenty, fifty, or one hundred years ago, we can't assume that's how he will currently move. If we do, we could miss Him. We need to let God show us what revival looks like in our present time. We need to let Him show us what His glory looks like in the context of our life.

I remember when I first began experiencing the Lord, there were several preachers who I looked up to. Even though God was greatly using them and I deeply admired them, I knew I needed to make the decision to not try to be exactly like these other preachers. I needed to be like me. That's not to say that I couldn't learn from them; it's that we need to remember that God wants to show His glory in the context of who *we* are.

Sometimes we can get in mindsets like, "I want to prophesy like so-and-so," or "I want to preach just like my favourite speaker." Don't make it your goal to prophesy like someone else. Don't try to speak just like those who you respect. Prophesy like you. Speak like you. Allow God to show you how to find your voice. Discover what the glory of God looks like in the context of your life. The truth is this: when you see who God is, you understand who you are. This is where we are able to relax in our gifting and find our voice. We can do this because we've found our confidence in Him.

God wants to encounter you with His glory. He wants His glory to linger upon you. Just as God called me to the dark nations, He wants to teach you to shine brightly in dark places. He wants to make you a beacon of revival.

The Father of glory wants to encounter you.

— Charlie Robinson

"God is looking for those who will believe in who the word says He is. He is one who longs to outpour His love on the earth. His heart is for revival. God is looking for those who will root themselves in intimacy with Him. He is looking for those who will be faithful in stewarding their flame."

— *Jerame Nelson*

The Outpourings of God
By: Jerame Nelson

We have been experiencing revival in San Diego for over one thousand days straight.

In 2016, my wife, Miranda, and I were in Pasadena attending a conference. James Goll, a known prophet to the nations, was speaking. During his message, led by the Holy Spirit, he pointed my wife and me out in the crowd. What we didn't realize, was that he was going to give us a prophetic word that would be the catalyst of something that would change our lives.

He said, "I see a West Coast rumble of revival. You are going to see a move of God. It will start in San Diego."

The next weekend in San Diego, Miranda and I were putting on a conference of our own. To say God's presence showed up powerfully would be an understatement. God's presence wasn't only powerful, it was electric. It was like we were living under a funnel from heaven, allowing us to continually experience the glory of

God. We witnessed what felt like countless miracles breaking out. Even though it isn't uncommon for us to experience the miraculous, I remembered the word that James had given us the week prior. Something unique was taking place. I knew in my spirit that God didn't want what was happening to end. We went on the word of the Lord and extended the meetings. God was true to His word and kept showing Himself in significant ways. People continued getting healed, saved, and delivered.

Currently, over one hundred nations—including every state in America, and every province in Canada—have been represented in the revival we've been experiencing. Thousands of miracles have taken place. People have been healed of Lyme disease, cancer, and HIV. People have been lifted out of wheelchairs, stutters have ceased, and smell and taste have returned to people who had lost it. In the presence of God, metal pins and screws have melted and dissolved from bodies. I know this isn't only taking place in San Diego through Miranda, myself, and our team; many are experiencing an outpouring of heaven throughout the world. I undeniably know we are living in times of revival.

Take a look at this verse with me:

Acts 2:17-21: "And it shall come to pass in the last days, says God, that I will pour out of My Spirit on all flesh; your sons and your daughters shall prophesy, your young men shall see visions, your old men shall dream dreams. And on My menservants and on My maidservants I will pour out My Spirit in those days; and they shall prophesy. I will show wonders in heaven above and signs in the earth beneath: blood and fire and vapor of smoke. The sun shall be turned into darkness, and the moon into blood, before the coming of the great and awesome day of the Lord.

And it shall come to pass *that* whoever calls on the name of the Lord shall be saved."

This verse clearly shows us what revival looks like. In fact, it is the very DNA of revival. Revival is the outpourings of God. What does outpouring looking like, you ask? It looks like dreams, visions, and prophecy. It looks like healings, signs, wonders, and salvations. This verse is the clearest blueprint of revival I've found in the Bible. It doesn't say that in the last days God will pour out programs. It doesn't say that in the last days God will pour out CDs or DVDs. It says God will pour out His Spirit. In San Diego, we've tried to do everything in our power to pull on this outpouring from heaven. We want to see it last. We want to host God's presence so we can experience and facilitate the *more* of God.

Something I've learned is that outpouring can be birthed in a single moment. All it takes is one touch from God. Over my years in ministry, I've done several trips to Indonesia. On my second trip, I was invited to speak in a city called Manado. I wasn't given much information about the event I was speaking at. In all honesty, I thought I was just going to a regular church meeting, or perhaps a gathering for pastors. When I arrived, I was dumbfounded to realize I wasn't speaking at a small meeting at all; I was speaking at a stadium the size of a soccer arena. Not only that, but it was a stadium filled with five thousand Muslims!

I remember panic flooding me as I saw the ocean of people waiting to hear from me. I prayed to God, saying, "Lord, what should I do?"

He immediately spoke back to me, saying, "When you go up onto the stage, guarantee them that the first five deaf people who walk onto the stage will be healed. If they aren't healed, then I am not real."

"God I can't do that…" I stuttered.

He said, "Why not?"

"I've never done that before," I replied.

He said, "You told me that you would do anything for me. You said you would do it anytime and anywhere. I'm taking you up on your word."

Nervously, I went up on the stage knowing I was about to deliver a bold word. I stood before five thousand people who didn't yet know Jesus. I said, "The first five deaf people who come up onto this platform will get healed. If they aren't healed, my God is not real."

When the words left my mouth, I prayed internally, "Oh God, please let there be five deaf people here right now…"

Immediately responding, five deaf people came up onto the stage. Walking over to the first person, I laid my hand over their ear. As I prayed, their ear opened. They were completely healed. I prayed for the second, and their ear opened. The third was healed. The fourth was healed. I was blown away at the goodness of God!

The fifth person who waited for prayer was a little girl about eight years old. The girl's hair was covering the side of her face, preventing me from seeing her ear. I laid my hand on the side of her head. What I didn't know was that this girl had no eardrum, earlobe, or even a canal. Instead of an ear, all that she had was a deformed stretch of skin on the side of her head. I prayed that her deaf ear would open. When I removed my hand, God had given her a brand-new ear! It went from a deformed stretch of skin to a full ear with an eardrum, earlobe, and a canal!

Considering many people knew of this little girl who was born without an ear, all of the Muslims were baffled by the power of God. The place was in full-blown pandemonium. Some screamed; others wept. Miracles broke loose everywhere amongst the people. At the sight of the healing, faith in the power of Jesus came upon people. Without anyone even praying for them, two men stood up from their wheelchairs—completely healed. Out of the five thousand, a few thousand of them gave their hearts to the Lord.

After this meeting, word began spreading throughout Indonesia about the healings that took place. Due to what occurred, I was contacted to meet the governor and several of his officials the following day. Apparently, they were deeply moved by the testimony of the young girl who was given a new ear in the presence of God. When I went to the man's home, I wasn't surprised to see that he lived in a mansion. What did surprise me, however, was how God was turning this trip into something far more impactful than I ever could have expected. The masses were healed the night prior; the following day we would be having another crusade meeting. To top it off, here I was meeting with some of the top government leaders in Manado. I didn't know what I was supposed to do with these men and women. All I knew was that the Lord spoke one word to me for when I was with them. He said I was to, "Prophesy."

Standing before the governor and his officials, I was given a microphone and moved in faith and obedience to what the Lord had spoken to me. I began to prophesy over him and the officials who were with him. I said, "The Lord just showed me that there is around two hundred fifty million dollars that is about to come into your economy in the next three months."

I continued, saying, "This is going to take place because there is a natural glory in this region that people are drawn to."

When I prophesied this, the governor began to shake in the presence of God. Here he was, a Muslim man encountering the presence of Jesus. He didn't know what to do. The word I gave was confirmed when I was told afterwards that Manado has the largest attraction for underwater diving in the world. Not only that, but they were about to host the World Ocean Conference. Through this event they were estimating they would bring in two-hundred-and-fifty million dollars.

After giving the word, the governor said to me, "I undeniably know that you hear from God. My best friend owns the television stations throughout Indonesia. I want your crusade taking place tomorrow to be on secular television. Over two million people will be watching."

The next night, ten thousand people came out to the crusade instead of five thousand. Not only that, but this service was being filmed to be broadcast on every secular television channel. Wild miracles broke out that night. In the meeting alone, five thousand people gave their hearts to the Lord. Only God knows who was watching on television and gave their lives to Him from their homes.

This was one of the first crusades I had ever spoken at. Revival touched down in that region, resulting in me returning nine more times in only three years. Considering how God moved, the Muslim government opened up meetings for us. All of a sudden, we weren't doing ministry through the churches; we were doing it through the government! Through this, I was able to go on MTV to preach the gospel to the whole region. We saw what felt like innumerable healings, deliverances, and salvations. Revival in a region broke out because one eight-year-old girl was touched by God.

Another time, I was preaching in Ottawa, Ontario, in Canada. While I was preaching, there was a woman at the back of the church who caught my eye throughout the duration of the service. I could tell the Lord was highlighting her to me. Not seated in a pew, she was lying on a mat throughout all of worship and my speaking. What I wasn't aware of was that she was so sick that she couldn't even sit up straight on a chair. She had been fervently praying for a touch from God.

As the service concluded, the leaders helped the woman by bringing her up to me. They shared with me that she was diagnosed with a very aggressive stage four cancer, which had plagued her entire body. She didn't have much time left to live.

By faith, I laid hands on her and all I said was, "In Jesus' name." She came under the power of God and went down like a sack of potatoes. I went on, praying over others, believing that the woman had received a healing touch from Jesus.

A few days later, this woman got medical reports back confirming that she was instantly healed of stage four cancer. Not a trace of it was left in her body. The doctors were baffled, saying she was a medical marvel. Due to her radical healing, her entire family was saved. It birthed a move of God in Ottawa. For one hundred ninety nights we experienced a move of revival. On the streets, we saw over two thousand decisions for Jesus.

People often ask me what some of the keys of revival are. One key I learned when I was first saved. When I first met Jesus, the Lord spoke to me, saying, "Simply focus on the gospel." He told me that Jesus is revival, and that if I wanted to see revival then I needed to live the way He did. So, this is what I did. I went after the model of Jesus. I did what He said to do in Matthew 10:8, which says, "Heal the sick, cleanse the lepers, raise the dead, cast out demons. Freely you have received, freely give." A year and a half after getting saved, I was thrust into the nations to see revival. I believe this was the fruit of not allowing myself to get distracted. I dedicated my life to keeping my focus on Jesus.

Another essential key to revival is intimacy with God—cultivating a life of experiencing His presence. When I first met the Lord, I would spend hours and hours with Him. I would read the Bible and go for walks with Him. This has never changed for me. I'm still prioritizing the same thing: the presence of God, knowing Him, and trying my best to be obedient.

I have often said that intimacy with God and obedience to His Word release the manifestation of His kingdom. I don't seek God for power. I don't seek Him for gifts or messages. I seek Him to know Him. Everything flows from this place. I make sure I'm walking with Jesus. I make sure I'm having conversations with God every day. I think we can sometimes get so mystical that we miss the simplicity of intimacy—the simplicity of the gospel. If we can cultivate a lifestyle of communication with God, we will always have everything we need. It's in this place where we learn to prioritize the presence of God above gifting.

If you want to experience revival, you can't lean on a gift; you need to lean on the King. Everyone has a gift, but when the glory of God shows up we need to learn how to submit our gift to the King. It is all about the presence of the Lord. With us hosting revival in San Diego, we aren't primarily trying to minister to people. We are ministering to the presence—to the King. If we can learn to do that, God will heal those who need healing. He will deliver those who need deliverance. He will touch everyone who needs to be touched. The reason why most people don't experience revival is because they think it's about their gift. They think it has to do with them, when in reality we are just the donkey.

Zechariah 9:9: "Rejoice greatly, O daughter of Zion! Shout, O daughter of Jerusalem! Behold, your King is coming to you; He *is* just and having salvation, lowly and riding on a donkey, a colt, the foal of a donkey."

We need to remember that we can't see revival in and of ourselves. We need Him. We are the donkey that the King rides in on. Our gift is the donkey. In order to understand this, it takes humility. It takes unflinching obedience. When we posture ourselves in this way, we can truly be used. We won't submit to our own will, but His instead. This is when He can trust us. The glory of God comes and He can entrust us with something sustainable.

Revival is something that we initiate with God. We need to seek His face. James 4:8 says, "Draw near to God and He will draw near to you." There is a responsibility on mankind to seek His face and to seek righteousness. To those of us who make time to draw near to Him, there is a God attraction that comes upon us. That's how I've gotten what I've gotten; I have never stopped seeking His face ever since I've been saved. I have never stopped pressing in to know Him. I've also sacrificed time, money, relationships—whatever it takes—in order for my heart to be in the posture to know Him and to expand His kingdom on the earth.

In 2006 I was in Quebec ministering. Many don't know this, but Quebec is the least evangelized province in North America. The facility that held the conference sat seven hundred people, but there was less than one hundred in the room. At the time, I was still very new in ministry. I spoke the first night of the conference. I remember trying to speak and it felt much harder than I was used to. People had their arms crossed; some scowled. I could feel their resistance and criticisms. It felt like my words were falling right to the ground. I quickly realized that most of these people weren't even listening to me.

Standing before the crowd, I prayed, "God what do I do?"

God immediately responded, saying, "There is someone in the room who is completely deaf and needs a miracle. If you call them up for healing, I will break this meeting right open."

I stopped preaching and said, "I want anyone who is deaf to come up to the front right now. God wants to heal right now."

A little girl who was about seven years old came forward with her parents. Both her parents were already crying as they came to the front with their daughter. I didn't even ask what was wrong with her, knowing she was the one who was deaf.

I spoke in declaration, saying, "Deaf ears open in Jesus' name."

Right then, the presence of God slammed down on her and she was completely healed. What I didn't know was that this girl was born completely without eardrums in either ear. We had just witnessed a creative miracle. When this happened, those who were apathetic in the meeting were instantly engaged. The ninety people in the room began to scream and shout because of what God just did. Many cried and wept. Once that happened, I was so moved by what God did that I couldn't even preach anymore. We went right back into worship for the rest of the evening.

The next evening, instead of ninety people, seven hundred showed up to the meeting. This church hadn't been packed like this in thirty years. This one miracle actually birthed multiple ministries and churches in Quebec. Pastors began working together again. This one miracle actually shifted the whole province of Quebec.

Another time, I was ministering and received a word of knowledge about someone who had lost their sense of taste and smell. A girl stood up saying it was her. I began to pray over her, and right on the spot God gave her sense of smell back. She began to weep.

I felt like the Lord said to me, "Give her some candy to get her to test her sense of taste."

I gave her some candy and she began to bawl all the more. She realized that God hadn't only given her sense of smell back, but her ability to taste as well!

I felt like the Lord told me to ask her how she lost her sense of smell and taste. She explained that when she was eight years old, her father who is no longer in her life punched her so hard that it knocked all of her senses out. This prevented her from tasting and smelling.

Once she was healed, she said to the whole church, "This is the first time since I was eight years old that I've felt the Father's love." With tears in her eyes, she said, "I want to forgive my dad right now."

This wrecked the whole room, including me. Everyone was weeping. Everyone in the room began forgiving their fathers and those who had hurt them from their pasts. It was one of the most amazing meetings and realms of glory I have seen.

As I mentioned before, revival is something that we initiate with God. God is looking for those who will be faithful in their pursuit of Him. He is looking for those who will steward their fire well. One of the things the Lord spoke to me not too long ago was about the ministry of faithfulness. Years ago, the Lord gave me a very interesting revelation concerning this from His Word.

Acts 1 shares a story about how a new apostle would need to be chosen to replace Judas. Lots were cast for the position between two men: Justus and Matthias. The requirements for who would be chosen to become an apostle weren't what we would assume. It didn't say they needed to have performed great miracles, signs, or wonders. It didn't say they needed to have prophesied great mysteries. They didn't need to have done some great exploit. The requirement was that they had to have been present since the baptism of John, all the way until their present time. They needed to understand faithfulness. Out of that place of faithfulness there were two men who fit the criteria. The lots were cast, and Matthias was appointed as one of the twelve apostles. He rose to position and favour because of his diligence in being faithful.

Some time ago, God gave me a vision. I saw into heaven where I saw twelve stones. These stones were set up as memorials, each had one of the apostles' names written upon it. There is a stone in heaven that has Matthias' name on it. There is no great exploit of his that we have a record about, yet there is a stone with his name on it. I believe God did this on purpose because one of the foundation stones of heaven is being faithful. Matthias' great exploit was his faithfulness. That is Matthias' story. This is how we can look at small things and not grow weary. Faithfulness releases breakthrough on the earth. Even if we are in a season where we maybe aren't seeing as much, we need to remember the value of faithfulness. I believe that faithfulness is one of the greatest keys that this next generation needs to understand.

God is looking for those who will believe in who the Word says He is. He is one who longs to outpour His love on the earth. His heart is for revival. God is looking for those who will root themselves in intimacy with Him. He is looking for those who will be faithful in stewarding their flame. He is looking for those who will understand that intimacy with God and obedience to His Word in faithfulness, together release the manifestation of His kingdom on the earth.

— Jerame Nelson

JAMIE GALLOWAY

Jamie Galloway carries a revival message that imparts a lifestyle of the supernatural. After receiving a powerful encounter with God, Jamie Galloway immediately began an incredible journey into the supernatural. During this time, God began using Jamie in some very unusual ways while giving him a love for the word of God, and a rich level of communion with Jesus. He ministers, speaking nationally and internationally and is currently involved in various media projects that highlight the supernatural move of the Holy Spirit.

"Revival is about a homecoming to the Father. It's about sons and daughters being immersed in His love for them."

— Jamie Galloway

The Father's Heart
By: Jamie Galloway

It's important for us to understand the heart of revival. We often talk about revival as though it's a chance for us to renew our faith. It's true that our faith is renewed; but it's so much more. Revival is about a homecoming to the Father. It's about sons and daughters being immersed in His love for them.

When I was twenty-two years old, I had the honour of being part of an internship under a man named Randy Clark. This internship changed my life. It taught me about the heart of the Father and integrity in revival. As an intern, I would be invited from time to time to speak and minister at different churches and conferences. One time in particular, I was invited to minister at a youth retreat in Ohio. This youth group was in a small town. The church hosting me was filled with very good and genuine people.

On my way to the retreat, I was with a man named Jerry Niswander who was a part of the pastoral team of the church. On the drive, I remember him turning to me, saying, "Jamie, I don't know if we can get to the meeting. The roads are flooded."

Immediately, I began thinking of this from a prophetic point of view. I know that often as things are in the natural realm, so are they in the spiritual. I said, "Jerry, I think this means there is going to be an outbreak of the Spirit."

I spoke these words in faith, but I didn't have a clue concerning the magnitude of how they would unfold.

We took some backroads, making it to where the retreat was being held. Arriving, I ministered, speaking to the youth for two days. In all honesty, those two days felt very normal. God was moving and touching hearts, but nothing was happening that I would consider out of the ordinary. That was, until the last hour of the retreat.

In the last hour, there was a deluge of the Spirit of God that broke out. Kids all over the room were crying and getting delivered from demons. Many were shouting and screaming at the top of their lungs. They were being set free from addictions and different things that tormented them. Many had received a touch from God like they had never experienced before. We had such a powerful time together.

Once I arrived home from the retreat, I was processing everything I had just experienced. There was something so real—so genuine—about how those youth were encountering God.

Not long after, I received a phone call from Jerry. He said, "We need you to come back again to our church in the next two weeks."

I appreciated that they wanted to have me back to speak, but I couldn't help but feel there was more to the story.

"What happened after I left?" I asked.

Jerry blurted out, "What happened to the youth is spreading throughout the entire church! The adults want from God what the youth received."

I could hear the hunger in Jerry's voice. Something significant was happening with this church. I went back to minister, knowing that God was doing something unique. This was a traditional church, filled with people who wanted a genuine touch from heaven. They were so impacted by all their kids encountering God's heart for them. I didn't know what to expect of my time with them; however, I know God meets us when we are hungry. When the service began, I was surprised to see that the church was standing room only. From wall to wall, it was jam packed with people who wanted a taste of what the youth had experienced.

The first night while ministering, I felt like the Lord told me there was someone in the room who had a busted-up shoulder. Once I called out the word of knowledge, a teenage boy put up his hand saying it was him. In front of everyone, God touched this young boy's shoulder and completely healed him.

What I later found out, was that this boy was the quarterback for the high school football team. For those of you who don't know American football, this is the type of city in Ohio where if you are the high school quarterback, you are essentially the celebrity of the town. That said, as soon as people saw him healed, everyone wanted what he had received. They all wanted a taste of what heaven was pouring out. We went into three solid weeks of outpouring. People were healed of lifelong traumas; some were freed from addictions. People were healed of multiple sclerosis; some were lifted out of wheelchairs. The healings that took place were absolutely amazing.

One day, I walked into the church office and there were over a dozen pairs of eyeglasses sitting in a box on a desk. Many of them were thick like coke-bottle glasses. I asked one of the pastors, "What are all these reading glasses for? Are you guys taking a collection for people who can't see?"

He replied, "No, people are leaving these behind at the church as they're healed in the presence of God."

One of the amazing things about this was that no one would even pray for their sight to be restored. Many would get healed during the worship and the message. Others would come up to the altar at the end of the service and leave their glasses up at the front because they were completely healed.

As God poured out in this church, we saw well over two hundred salvations in only three weeks. Even drug dealers in the town were getting saved. One of the phenomena that took place was people walking into the church because they saw a light hovering over the building. They didn't know why they would see this light so they would just come in. This would often result in them getting saved.

We knew we couldn't stop doing these meetings because people were begging for more of Jesus. We had one night that was very special. The local deaf community, which consisted of about thirty people, came out to the church. They did something that was absolutely remarkable. Without even the pastor's permission, each one went up on the stage and simultaneously began worshipping in sign language. This was a testament of how dynamic the unity in that room was in the Spirit.

Randy Clark ended up coming out to the move of God taking place. When he saw what was happening, he began to cry, saying something I'll never forget. He said, "In all my years of revival I've never seen anything like this."

Seeing his reaction, I knew this was real deal revival. Randy Clark is the one who imparted to me the integrity of revival. Being one of the fathers of the Toronto Airport Renewal, this man knows what he's talking about. What we were experiencing wasn't hyped up; it wasn't fabricated. We tried our best to protect this move of God so we could keep it pure. It would have been hard to hype up because it was so genuine.

Over the years, I remember times being in church services with Randy that would be considered by most as something to qualify for extended meetings. He would walk away from those meetings saying, "This is good, but it isn't it."

Being a younger man, I would be like, "Why aren't we going into extended meetings when eighty percent of the people were healed?"

He would say, "Yup, but that's not it."

Randy imparted to me the understanding that when we are talking about revival, it better be revival. We don't want to make things look like something is happening if it's not. We want to speak in faith, but we don't want to speak in vanity. We need to be honest about what God is doing. It's fine to say, "God is moving," but we can't fabricate revival. The momentum of revival is when people are being so impacted that they're being launched into full-time ministry or people are moving geographically to experience what God is pouring out. If we are making statements, then what we are experiencing better be worthy of what we are saying because it can affect people's lives.

I'm so thankful for the fathers and mothers that God has brought around me over the years, like Randy. I'm thankful that God works by bringing generations together. Psalm 68:4-6 says, "Sing to God, sing praises to His name; extol Him who rides on the clouds, by His name Yah, and rejoice before Him. A father of the fatherless, a defender of widows, *is* God in His holy habitation. God sets the solitary in families…"

When we learn to encounter the Father's heart, He aligns us for revival. He positions us so we are readied to experience Him in fullness. We can see in Psalm 68:4-6, that the Father brings us into family. I believe this is a pivotal revelation for stewarding our own heart revival. In fact, if I were to ever be able to speak to my younger self, I would say, "Learn the power of relationships. Learn to be a friend. Learn to invest in others."

If I want to have revival in my life, I need to stay refreshed. A part of that is inviting the Father to bring people around me. It's being willing to invest in others. It's investing into others like I would want to be invested in myself. I have friends who refresh and revive me. Some of these people have never even been to my meetings. Revival is about a lot more than just having good meetings, it's about experiencing the kingdom outside as well. Kingdom relationships are the Father's heart for us.

Kingdom relationships position us for greatness; they position heaven to move on the earth. In fact, whenever

God is about to do something, we always see generations coming together in relationship. We can see this in Jesus' life while He walked the earth. Jesus was someone who was tremendously intentional with having people around Him. After Jesus was baptized, He went to the wilderness for forty days. Once He emerged, He found His disciples. It's important to note that Jesus didn't do much ministry before this. It seems like He didn't experience the double portion in his ministry until He elected His disciples to follow him. Right when Jesus surrounded Himself with those who He could invest in, the Father launched Him!

We need to learn how to partner with the generations who have gone before us, and those who are coming after. We can see in scripture that Jesus called the disciples to Himself. He didn't wait for them to come to Him; He sought them out. I've unfortunately seen people's ministries held back because they haven't been pouring out into those who were to come after them. I've then seen them skyrocket once they've surrounded themselves with those who they could pour into. You can't minister to the crowd until you have the one-on-ones.

The revival we experienced in Ohio lasted for months, resulting in this five-hundred-person church becoming a megachurch. This was my earliest taste of revival. This was the launching point for everything I do in ministry. I was invited as an intern, and then bam! God launched me. In going to minister at this church, I wasn't looking to gain anything from it. I wasn't longing for platform; I was just wanting to pour out and train God's people. However, this is what happens in revival. People are transformed, raised up, and sent out. We saw many profound leaders come out of this move of God who are still doing great things to advance the kingdom on the earth.

One of the greatest things I took away from this move of God was what it was all based around: a revelation of the Father's love. This was the message that was being imparted to the people—"Father God loves you. Papa God loves you."

When we are hosting the presence of God, we need to remember to keep the main thing the main thing. We can't get caught up in the weeds. When we are talking about the message of the kingdom and who God is, we can't get caught up focusing on random things that aren't going to increase the understanding of the awareness of the presence of God. Historically, we can see revivals where God is moving, but then people begin to lose their fire. I believe this happens because we can have a tendency to try and define the revival according to a specific doctrine that has greatly impacted us. We put a distinct focus on a particular theology or elementary principle, instead of keeping it about the Father's goodness. We can get caught up saying things like, "There's a specific angel that is being released in this revival..." or, "This revival is marked by a specific manifestation..." What we don't realize is that this can deter us from focusing on the goodness of God. When we try to complicate it, we can get distracted by the minor things. We end up focusing on what's secondary, when the Father just wants His kids to come home and be with Him. When we understand the Father's heart, we cultivate something that I believe is very significant. We cultivate compassion.

1 John 3:1: "Behold what manner of love the Father has bestowed on us, that we should be called children of God!"

Mark 6:34: "And Jesus, when He came out, saw a great multitude and was moved with compassion for them, because they were like sheep not having a shepherd. So He began to teach them many things."

Matthew 14:14: "And when Jesus went out He saw a great multitude; and He was moved with compassion for them, and healed their sick."

Last year, I was speaking in a meeting. There was a lady who came into the church. Unable to walk herself, she was wheeled in by a few men in a cart. This poor woman hadn't walked for six years. While I was ministering, this woman sat listening intently. My eyes kept being drawn to her over and over again. It bothered me that she hadn't walked for so long. As each minute passed, compassion was filling my heart for her.

I find it very interesting that in Mark 6:34, it doesn't say that Jesus was moved by an open vision or the word of the Lord. It says He was moved by compassion. As I looked at this woman, I found myself feeling upset that she couldn't walk. I asked some of the men in the meeting to help lift her up. In front of the whole church, I got them to lift her as she tried to move her feet. The whole church was praying and believing. After about thirty minutes, she did not walk. It was hard to see because we were all believing by faith for her. I couldn't leave this woman as she was. I knew it was the character of God to heal. I needed to stir up hope. I felt like I had a responsibility to prophesy.

Into the microphone, I said, "Everyone, watch. Tomorrow she will walk."

I knew I was triggering something in the spirit. God wanted this woman to walk again.

The next day, I was flying home and I got a Facebook message. The message had a video of the woman who hadn't walked for six years. Her husband was filming her as she walked throughout her house from one side to the other, completely healed!

I believe this is the type of tenacity of faith that is required if we are going to see revival; but it's a tenacity sparked by compassion. We will often wait to move because we are waiting for God's word to be proclaimed, but what if it's that He is waiting for our compassion? We need to have compassion for those around us. We need to have compassion for those who are being tormented. We need compassion for cities and nations. I love the spectacular things—the supernatural—but I feel there is something about human emotion that God is waiting on. He is waiting on our compassion. I believe this is an irreplaceable key to the miraculous.

I was recently ministering in Montana. In the meeting I felt compassion coming upon me for those who needed healing in their eyes. There was a woman whose eyesight was so bad that when she would look at someone, they looked like a blob. When prayed for, Jesus gave her complete sight! For the first time that she could remember, she could see people clearly. My team and I prayed for every blind person and we watched as every one of them was healed. While ministering in Edmonton, something similar happened. This time, I felt compassion stirring in me for those who needed restoration for hearing. My team and I prayed for every deaf person and they were all healed. These healings weren't only due to faith; it was compassion that sparked revival.

Matthew 4:17: "From that time Jesus began to preach and to say, "Repent, for the kingdom of heaven is at hand."

We often have ebbs and flows in our lives because we are pressing in for an invisible thing; we are pressing in for an infinite thing. We need to allow God to renew our minds so we can be attuned to heaven. He wants us to understand that the kingdom of heaven is at hand; revival is at hand. It's in this place where the impossible can take place. We carry the spirit of revival by talking about God's goodness, by living a life of repentance, and by being set apart. For me, I've needed to learn to steward my heart culture so that even when I'm not in the atmosphere of revival, I'm still experiencing it. If revival is occurring in my heart, it doesn't matter what's going on around me. I'm in a lot of church meetings, some being more dynamic than others. This is why revival can't be only about hosting meetings. It's about hosting revival in your heart. This is where the pivotal key of compassion blooms.

Revival is the overflow of our heart culture; our heart culture is determined by us encountering the Father's love for us. When we live in this place of the Father's love and external revival comes, we will fit it like a glove. We aren't stuck thinking, "I need to make a major shift in my life," because we are already living in it. We won't need to shift because we are there every day. When we do this, we move into revival with grace and ease.

I believe we are living in a time where the Father wants to pour out His love on the earth. He wants to pour it over your your family, city, and nation. He's declaring a homecoming for sons and daughters to encounter His heart for them. The Father is declaring revival. He wants to birth revival around you. He wants to birth revival through you.

As I said before, the revival we experienced in Ohio was all based around one truth alone. This truth is something that God was declaring over all of those youth, and it's something that He is declaring over you now. That truth is this:

"Father God loves you. Papa God loves you."

— Jamie Galloway

JOAN HUNTER

Joan Hunter ministers the gospel with manifestations of supernatural signs and wonders in healing schools, miracle services, conferences, and churches around the world. Her focus is to train and equip believers to take the healing power of God beyond the four walls of the church and to the four corners of the earth. Joan is a compassionate minister, a dynamic teacher, an accomplished author, and an anointed healing evangelist. She has ministered in countries all over the world and has made numerous television and radio appearances. She has authored more than twenty-two books and has recorded teachings that will encourage you and teach you how to pray for the sick and see them recover. Joan Hunter and her husband, Kelley, live northwest Houston, TX. Together, they have four daughters, four sons, three sons-in-law, and seven grandchildren. Joan is the daughter of the Happy Hunters, Charles & Frances Hunter.

"When Jesus comes to abide within us, all power of heaven and earth comes in as well. Therefore, whether we are declaring life or death, whatever comes out of our mouth has that same power. If we want to see our lives in alignment, then we need to get our mouth in alignment."

— Joan Hunter

Healing and Wholeness
By: Joan Hunter

Revival isn't supposed to last for only one generation. God's heart is for generations to work together, so that when fathers and mothers pioneer something in the spirit, sons and daughters will carry on what God has done through them. Honouring those who have gone before us isn't simply speaking good of them; it's also about standing upon the foundation they've built and advancing God's kingdom. We need to do this so that those who come after us can stand on what we've built and go further than we ourselves have gone.

I have the honour of being the daughter of Charles and Frances Hunter, known as the "Happy Hunters." My mom and dad spent nearly forty years leading "Healing Explosions," where they prayed for the sick and taught about the ministry of healing throughout the world. They paved the way for many people. I travelled with them for about thirty years. Many people will ask me what I've seen; and it's a valid question because the healing that took place through their ministry was amazing. I learned a lot and saw a lot.

Mom and Dad played a huge role in bringing a revelation of Mark 16:17-18 to the church, which says, "And these signs will follow those who believe: In My name they will cast out demons; they will speak with new tongues; they will take up serpents; and if they drink anything deadly, it will by no means hurt them; they will lay hands on the sick, and they will recover."

When we would go into a city, my parents wanted to not only demonstrate healing; they also wanted to train people to walk in it. About twenty or thirty churches would be involved in a city crusade. They would help gather five hundred people to teach them and train them in healing. We would then have large gatherings from anywhere between five thousand and fifteen thousand people. The amazing thing was that the people who were trained in healing were the ones who would do the praying. We would do these at least once a month and remarkable healings would take place. People would rise up out of wheelchairs. Blind eyes would open. The deaf would hear. We would see thousands upon thousands of people miraculously healed.

People didn't only receive teaching and training on healing; they saw it with their own eyes. They saw Jesus heal others through their own hands! This way, when they are going about their day and they see someone in pain, it's natural for them to pray for them and see them healed. This didn't only result in people being trained or healed, it also changed cities.

My parents walked in a remarkable healing anointing that was primarily physical. I am so thankful for what I received through them, and I'm thankful that I've gotten to build on the foundation they had laid. Through my own journey, God has given me what I believe is a pivotal key to healing. This key is learning to allow God to not only heal our body, but also our heart.

I love sharing my personal story, because I've learned that it's so important that when we get healed, we give our testimony. Revelation 19:10 says, "For the testimony of Jesus is the spirit of prophecy."

In 2000, I was faced with divorce after twenty-six years of marriage due to unfaithfulness on his part. It was completely devastating. I had been in full-time ministry for years, travelling with my parents, and pastoring. Not only did I lose my identity as his wife, but I also lost my identity as the co-pastor of our church. We lost our church and travelling ministry. We lost the house and our family unit. All our finances and income were gone. We literally lost everything. To say it plainly, I was a wreck.

After experiencing such pain in my family, I went to get my annual mammogram. I didn't think much of it going in. Everything was routine; yet, I had no clue that everything was about to change for me. I found out that my whole left side was full of cancer. My family had fallen apart and now I was faced with a life-threatening illness. I believe that all of the worry, stress, and trauma that I battled due to the divorce brought on the breast cancer.

With circumstances crashing in all around me, I couldn't help but take notice of something. There was no doubt that I was hurt by the cancer, but I was devastated by the divorce. I knew that I could live without a breast, but I couldn't live with a broken heart.

This was when I was faced with something that I didn't expect. Growing up with my mom and dad, I saw many physical healings, but they never really touched on things like fear, trauma, anxieties, stress, etc. It was true that I needed healing in my body, but it was undeniable that I needed a healing touch from God in my soul.

I thought to myself, "I can deal with the cancer afterwards, but now, I need to get my heart healed."

I learned very quickly that the counsellors I saw weren't trying to teach me how to be healed, they were trying to coach me to live with my pain. They would say, "In seven or eight years, you'll feel a little bit better; but you know you'll never fully get over this, don't you?"

I would hear this and think, "This isn't biblical... I've seen too much to believe what they are saying." I didn't want to learn to live with this; I wanted to be set free.

I went after God to heal my broken heart. I knew that He didn't want me to cope with the pain, He wanted to eradicate it.

I would tuck myself away with God. This may sound funny, but I would often have my alone time with Him in the shower. This was when my children would be taken care of and the demands of life were outside the door. I was free to be alone with Him. I was determined to get healed. Even though I was diagnosed with broken heart syndrome and had been given a death sentence of cancer, I allowed my faith to grow. While the water would wash over me, I would allow the truth of God's Word to wash over me. His truth would come over me and heal me. He taught me to forgive. I needed to forgive my ex-husband. I realized that when I released him, I was actually releasing myself into healing and freedom. I asked the Father to heal me of unforgiveness, betrayal, abandonment, and rejection.

I would declare over myself, saying, "I will live and not die, and declare the works of the Lord."

Doing this time and time again, I noticed that the heaviness I was feeling in my heart began to lift. God was healing my heart and removing the trauma.

Over time, I remember thinking to myself, "It's about time for me to go to the oncologist again. I need to see how I'm doing physically."

I went into the doctor's office and after two hours of examination and a gallon of goop everywhere you can imagine, the nurses were like, "I thought the cancer was on the left side... Maybe it's on the right side?"

After checking the right side again, they said, "Let's try the left side again..."

They couldn't figure out what happened to my cancer. It was completely gone!

I realized that when my heart was healed, so was my body. I learned how to literally starve my sickness to death.

Starving your sickness to death starts with your mouth. Proverbs 18:21 says, "Death and life *are* in the power of the tongue, and those who love it will eat its fruit." We need to learn to watch what we are speaking over ourselves. We shouldn't be speaking over ourselves things such as: "I'll never get out of debt. I'll never be happy. I'll always be anxious. I'll never get healed. The doctor says I only have two years to live, so it must be true." We need to agree with what God's Word says. We need to be speaking over ourselves that, "Jesus is my healer. He is my provider. He is my joy. He is my peace." When Jesus comes to abide within us, all power of heaven and earth comes in as well. Therefore, whatever comes out of our mouth has that same power, whether we are declaring life or death. If we want to see our lives in alignment with heaven, then we need to get our mouth in alignment first.

Here I am now, living out exactly what I spoke over myself. In the shower, in God's presence, I would say, "I will live and not die, and declare the works of the Lord." Twenty years later, here I am, living and whole. I'm living out the reality of my words.

I think we would be amazed if we knew how important a role trauma has in sickness and disease. Trauma is often the cause of those diseases. I've met many people who have had an accident, such as falling off of a ladder and hurting their shoulder. They will get prayed for and it will feel much better, but there's still a nagging pain. It's because the physical injury has been addressed, but not the trauma. What we often don't realize is that when we experience trauma, our body stores the pain that we experienced at a cellular level. This is why when I pray for someone to be healed, I will often pray that the trauma will go from the cellular memory. This way we are dealing with the root of the pain.

Hebrews 8:12: "For I will be merciful to their unrighteousness, and their sins and their lawless deeds I will remember no more."

The Word says that the Father remembers our sins no more. He actually *chooses* to remember our sins no more. One day I thought to myself, "If the Father can choose to remember our sins no more, then we can choose to forget the sins that we've done or have been done to us." This way we can actually be healed and set free at the very root of an issue.

I've found this to be helpful for many women who have been diagnosed with fibromyalgia. I was in a meeting not long ago and we had seventeen women lined up at the front who needed healing from fibromyalgia. This is an ailment which medically has no cure. It's widely known throughout medical communities that you can subdue this ailment with medication; but once stress comes in, it will resurface. What they don't realize is that this is happening because the root was never dealt with.

So here we were, seventeen women were lined up in front of an entire congregation. I went from woman to woman asking them the same question. "When were you diagnosed with fibromyalgia?"

No matter how long ago they were diagnosed, I would ask them, "What happened to you the year before you were diagnosed?"

Many of the women would break down crying, having experienced some form of intense trauma the year prior to their diagnosis. Some of them had been in traumatic car accidents; others experienced sexual abuse. Some experienced abandonment, severe rejection, or death of a family member. For each of these women, it was trauma that opened up the door to fibromyalgia.

When dealing with situations like this, we pray and deal with the spirit of trauma. We curse it, just like Jesus cursed the fig tree. We curse it to its very roots. From there, we curse the spirit of fibromyalgia, the spirit of pain, and chronic fatigue syndrome. We command them to leave in Jesus' name.

Every single one of these women had some sort of traumatic event take place the year before they were diagnosed. Every one of them was completely healed. Jesus didn't only heal bodies; He healed their broken hearts.

Another time, a mother and daughter came to me for prayer. The daughter was tormented by learning disabilities and was having a very hard time in school. I knew I could have just prayed for healing, but I had to get to the root of the issue. I knew that God wanted to set her completely free.

I said to her, "Do you know if there was anything traumatic that happened to her while she was in the womb while the brain was forming?"

Most people don't realize that it's very possible for us to have life-altering experiences in the womb. Scripture shows us this. Luke 1:41 says, "And it happened, when Elizabeth heard the greeting of Mary, that the babe (John the Baptist) leaped in her womb; and Elizabeth was filled with the Holy Spirit." John the Baptist literally leapt with joy in the womb when Jesus was near. Just as we can experience positive things in the womb, we can have negative experiences as well.

"Yes, she did have something traumatic happen..." the mother said quietly, replying to my question.

By her response and the look on her face, I knew I was about to hear an intense story.

"What happened?" I asked.

The mother said, "When I was five or six months pregnant, my husband came into the house with a gun. He was trying to aim for my stomach; at the baby. When he shot the gun, the bullet hit me in the shoulder instead. I collapsed onto the floor. I knew that I needed to pretend I was dead, or he would have shot me again. Thinking he had killed me and our child, he turned the gun on himself and ended his own life."

This young girl experienced great trauma in the womb, hindering her brain from fully developing. I had the privilege of praying for this young girl. We dealt with the trauma of what she experienced when she was in the womb and God completely healed her heart. As a result, her learning disabilities were healed! She is now thriving in school.

I met another man who was a Vietnam war veteran. This man battled post-traumatic stress disorder (PTSD). He was trained for war in such a way that if someone were to wake him up in the middle of the night, his first instinct would be to kill them, believing his life to be in danger. This was so severe that his wife would need to build a barrier of pillows between them as they slept so that she wouldn't accidently wake him up in the night. He battled PTSD for forty-three years. After receiving prayer for the trauma that he experienced during the war, he was completely healed of PTSD. Jesus healed his trauma, his mental illness, and even his memories from war.

I literally have tens of thousands of other testimonies just like these. People find it hard to believe that Jesus can do this because they don't think it can be this easy, but it is. This is the power of God moving in and through us. If you're reading this and you've wrestled with any form of trauma, depression, anxiety, self-hatred, or fear, remember that God wants to heal your heart. We should not choose to accept our wounds as a permanent condition. We have an opportunity to trust God for healing and deliverance. We can make the decision to begin chasing after our healing. Unfortunately, some of us have even adopted this condition as our identity. However, it's time for us to rip those labels off so we can be who God has created us to be. God's Word can break the chains off of us that hinder and oppress us. As they break off, we need to be sure not to pick them up again. Things like unforgiveness, betrayal, abandonment, rejection need to be left behind us. Those things aren't your portion anymore; complete healing is your new normal.

Not only does God want to heal us, He also wants to use us as vessels to heal others. What usually hinders us from praying for others is the fear that we will step out and nothing will happen. This fear is often rooted in the fear of rejection, believing that God doesn't want to use us. When we train people to pray for the sick, we work on getting rid of that fear. We teach people that it's our job to pray and God's job to heal. We pray in faith and we get to watch Him do the rest.

I always tell people that anyone can walk in the anointing that I walk in, because it's Jesus who is inside of me who does the healing. When people get that revelation, they have the faith to step out and do it. This is why I have such a heart for equipping people to do the works of ministry. I don't want to only demonstrate healing; I want to teach others how to do it as well. I have spent forty-seven years in the ministry of healing. I want to train people—younger people. I want to train people who are in their 20s, 30s, and 40s who can take this revelation and run with it for decades in the future!

You need to know that God has called you to minister to the sick. It doesn't matter what you've been through or where you came from. It doesn't matter whether you are the first believer in your family or not. In my case, I had parents who provided an amazing foundation for me; but, believe it or not, I'm actually not here because of who my parents were. I had to make a personal decision to follow the leading of God for my life. I had to make a decision to live a life of faith. It's a personal decision to say "yes" to Him. We need to run after the Father, and if we do He will turn our life around. He will inspire us. He will encourage us. He is the one who will take us from our current state to where He wants us to be—if we are willing.

Whatever Jesus did, you can do it too. Don't let anyone tell you that you can't. You are called, anointed, and appointed.

– Joan Hunter

BILL PRANKARD

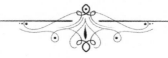

Bill Prankard, founder of the Bill Prankard Evangelistic Association, is a healing evangelist with a burning vision for revival. During his more than five decades of evangelistic ministry, Bill has taken healing and hope "from sea to sea" in Canada and abroad. Thousands of people have received outstanding physical miracles and spiritual transformations as he crosses denominational lines and carries the full gospel message. He has established and led churches, hosted weekly and daily television ministry, and authored several books and publications. At "the ends of the earth," in both the Canadian and Russian Arctic, he and his teams have taken the gospel where the name of Jesus had never been heard—mentoring leaders and spearheading the funding and establishment of native churches. Bill and his wife Gwen are parents to four adult married children, twelve grandchildren and eleven great-grandchildren.

"Anointing is no more and no less than relationship with Holy Spirit."

— Bill Prankard

Believing for Nations
By: Bill Prankard

I'm seventy-six years old this year. Throughout the years, I've laid down my life to live for revival. I've been involved with moves of God that feel like you're being spoiled in His presence. I've seen amazing things. With all I've experienced, there is a truth that burns deep within me that I believe with all my heart: we are at the beginning of the greatest revival. Not only that, but whoever wants to be a part of the *chosen generation*, will be right in the middle of what God is about to do.

I was brought up Anglican Christian and United—then baptized in water in the Baptist church. Even though I grew up immersed in church, I wouldn't say I knew Jesus. It wasn't until I was eighteen years old when I came into a Pentecostal church, got saved, and was filled with the Spirit. Almost immediately God called me into ministry. My wife, Gwen, and I got married young, had our kids young, and went into ministry young.

In the 1970s Gwen and I were pastoring a small church in the Ottawa Valley. At the time, there were busloads of people every week going to Pittsburgh, Pennsylvania. These people would drive twelve hours to attend a Friday morning miracle service led by a woman named Kathryn Kuhlman. I didn't know a lot about her at the time. I hadn't heard about the powerful anointing she walked in. I hadn't heard of the undeniable healings that took place in her ministry; but she piqued our curiosity. Growing up, my wife and I had watched Oral Roberts on television. We saw the miracles in the tent meetings that took place. As children, that put seeds of hunger within us. We knew miracles could happen.

Up until that point in our ministry, we believed in the miraculous but didn't often see it ourselves. We would pray for people and occasionally see them healed, but we never really knew if it was going to happen or not. One particular day, Gwen was listening to Kathryn Kuhlman's radio program and she was actually touched and healed through the radio. We were blown away! We had never experienced the power of God like that before. What we didn't realize was that Holy Spirit was in pursuit of us.

There was a man I met who had been healed at one of Kathryn's meetings. He invited me to come to one, saying he would love to bring a pastor with him. I was young— only twenty-seven years old at the time—and in all honesty, I was really struggling with something: I really wanted to go to the meeting, but I couldn't wrap my head around how someone would need to travel such a distance in order to see the power of God demonstrated.

There was a group of pastors who I looked up to at the time. I remember asking them, "Why is it that people need to travel so far to experience the power of God?"

They replied, saying, "You don't. Those people you're talking to are troubled. You need to stay far away from them. Those people could come to any of our churches and see the exact same thing." They then said, "You need to be careful of this *Kathryn Kuhlman*."

Even though I didn't realize it at the time, what this did was it put seeds of doubt inside my heart. Due to the opinions of the pastors I looked up to, I ended up growing very critical of Kathryn Kuhlman. I mean—I knew nothing about her other than the fact that my wife was healed through her radio program and that people were driving long distances to see her minister.

By the time I went down to Pittsburgh, Pennsylvania, for the miracle service, I didn't want to go. In my heart, I actually went there to criticize. So here I am, on a bus with these "troubled people" who I'm supposed to stay away from, to see Kathryn Kuhlman, who I was cautioned to be careful of. What I didn't realize was that my life was about to change forever. In my opinion, everything that has happened since 1972—everything that God has done in and through our ministry across Canada and the world—is because of what happened to me at that Friday morning meeting.

While I was sitting in the pew before the meeting began, there was a lady sitting next to me. She was a Catholic woman from Toronto. Seeing that I was a Pentecostal pastor, she leaned over to me, saying, "I'm so glad I'm sitting beside you, because you probably know all about this stuff. I've never even set foot in a Protestant church."

Back then, I was so arrogant and proud, thinking I knew everything. I thought to myself, "I agree with her, she's lucky to get to sit beside me."

The meeting began. Kathryn came onto the stage and it was unreal. She was dramatic and flamboyant. Although, what caught me off guard the most wasn't her demeanour; it was how overwhelmed I felt by the presence of God. When Kathryn began ministering to individual people, I was blown away. I had seen the occasional person fall when being prayed for, but people were literally being lifted off the ground and falling all over the place by the power of God!

All of a sudden, the Catholic lady grabbed my arm in fear, saying, "What is she doing to them?!"

I patted her shoulder and said to her, "Oh, don't worry, that's the power of God. It's okay."

When I said that, Holy Spirit came to me. I felt His finger in my chest. He said, "Yes, this is my power and you've never seen it. You've had a form of godliness and you've denied my power."

That was all it took for me to begin weeping. I don't normally cry like this, but I had my head in my knees, sobbing.

This lady who I'm supposed to be helping said to me, "Are you okay?"

Through my sobs, I said, "No..."

"Can I help you?" she asked.

I said, "No. No one can help me..."

I was weeping because I just discovered that I had been denying God's power. I was weeping because I realized I didn't know Holy Spirit. I had met Him; I'd received the baptism of the Holy Spirit and spoke in tongues, but I didn't know Him.

John 14:16-17: "And I will pray the Father, and He will give you another Helper, that He may abide with you forever—the Spirit of truth, whom the world cannot receive, because it neither sees Him nor knows Him; but you know Him, for He dwells with you and will be in you."

In John 14, Jesus was talking about this intimate thing that I realized I didn't have. I made two decisions that day. First, I would do my very best to never deny the power of God again. Second, I would give the rest of my life to intimately know Holy Spirit.

As I mentioned before, I'm seventy-six this year. In some ways, I feel like the apostle Paul. Towards the end of his ministry, Paul was still pursuing Holy Spirit. He said, "That I may know Him and the power of His resurrection," (Philippians 3:10). Paul pursued God until the end of his days. Ever since that moment, in a Friday morning miracle service, I've been on a pursuit to know Holy Spirit. He's my best friend. Everything that's happened in the ministry has been because of relationship with Him. When I teach about anointing, I make sure that people know it's not a force. Anointing is no more and no less than relationship with Holy Spirit.

In that meeting, I saw everything that I believe should happen if God truly is who He says He is. So many people were healed, delivered, and saved. This was a moment that would impact me for a lifetime. I remember coming out of the meeting, thinking to myself, "I hope I never have to talk about this. This is too sacred…"

Getting back on the bus, everyone looked stunned by what they had witnessed. However, I couldn't help but realize that no one in our group had gotten healed in the meeting. Before I could take a seat, I was greeted by the bus driver, Tom. On our way up, he promised he would come into the meeting; but just looking at him, I could tell he didn't set foot in the church.

"Tom, you should have come in. It was amazing!" I said to him.

He replied, saying, "If it was so amazing then why wasn't the little girl healed?"

I knew exactly what he was talking about.

My eyes rested on a little girl who was Greek Orthodox. She had come up with her mother. This poor little girl couldn't walk; her legs were like rubber. During the service, we had carried her into the church. We prayed and believed that God would heal her. If no one else was healed, we just wanted this little girl to be able to walk again. My heart sunk seeing her there on the bus, unhealed after I had experienced the power of God in such a profound way.

"I have no idea why she wasn't healed," was all I could say back to the bus driver.

I took a seat, wishing Tom could have experienced what I had; wishing the little girl had been healed that day. My eyes quickly grew heavy. We were all exhausted. We travelled twelve hours the day before, now we had to drive twelve hours home. As the bus started driving, I put my seat back and closed my eyes. This nap is where my ministry started.

After only being asleep for what felt like mere minutes, the man who organized the trip shook my shoulder, waking me up. Apparently, something was happening.

When I looked up, there were two Catholic ladies being touched by God; one of them was singing in the Spirit in tongues. She had never experienced anything like this before. The presence of God came into that bus in the exact way it fell in the service! I began walking up the aisle, when Holy Spirit told me that someone was being healed and told me exactly what they were being healed from.

I thought to myself, "What am I supposed to do with this?!"

Immediately, a lady grabbed my arm saying, "My friend has just been healed!" She went on to describe the exact same symptom that Holy Spirit had just revealed to me.

I went up to the front of the bus, grabbing the microphone. Pulling it up to my mouth, I said, "A lady has just been healed!"

The woman came up testifying of what God had just done. Just like that, we were going down the highway having a revival on the go! As she testified, the power of God hit her. No one was even praying for her and she fell right on her back in the aisle. You need to understand something: this was in March, so everything was slushy on the ground due to snow. No one in their right mind would willingly fall into all of that slush.

Everyone who was sleepy was instantly wide awake. All of a sudden someone else just shouted out, "I've just been healed!" One after another, people were getting healed and falling over into the slush.

I looked over at Tom, to see how he was responding to everything that was happening. He was driving down the highway, but he wasn't looking at the road. In the rear-view mirror, he was looking at the little girl running up and down the aisle of the bus, completely healed. People screamed, seeing that her legs were fully strong. Tom was weeping from what he was witnessing.

I was stunned, trying to facilitate this spontaneous outpouring of God's power. Since I was the one managing the microphone, someone came up to me saying, "When did this ministry start for you?"

The whole bus was in chaos. People were screaming and falling over. Our bus driver was lost in emotion from what was taking place. All I could reply was, "I have no clue, but we need to pray that someone knows how to drive a bus, otherwise this is going to go off the road and no one will ever know what God did on here!"

By the time we got home it seemed like everyone who needed healing was healed. I hadn't done anything other than just watch the power of God show up. Up until that point in my life, I had yearned for a healing ministry. I believed God could do it but hadn't seen such a demonstration of his power. Now I knew why; I had been pursuing a ministry, instead of pursuing a person. Here I was: I finally learned to pursue Holy Spirit and a healing ministry unfolded around me.

I'm amazed at the fruit that comes from moments like this. I actually received an email about ten years ago from a man. The email read: "You don't know me, but I just want you to know that what happened on that bus in 1972 is still happening today. Our family got saved from what happened that day and a number of us are in the ministry. Due to what happened, I never have a meeting where we don't minister to the sick. This all began on that bus. P.S. My dad was the bus driver."

The following Sunday after Kathryn Kuhlman's meeting, I knew what I needed to do. In front of the fifty people in our congregation, I repented. I said to them, "I've failed you and I've failed God. I've had a form of godliness, but I've denied God's power. I will never do it again."

I was just a mess. I wept before everyone, blubbering through the service. I didn't talk about healing or praying for the sick, but when the service concluded I was told by numerous people that they were healed throughout the meeting. These were people who in the past I had prayed for many times to be healed. I'm sure over the years I had poured so much oil over some of them that they were slippery, but they still didn't get healed!

That afternoon, I laid on my face before God in my office, overwhelmed by what He was doing. Considering what was happening, it was all I could bring myself to do. As night came around, I knew the evening service was about to begin. Coming out of my office, I saw that there were more people waiting in the lobby than usually came to church. The sanctuary was filled with people. The back rooms were filled. The whole place was jam packed!

As soon as I got up on the stage, I felt like Holy Spirit wanted to heal people, so I called it out in faith. People began getting healed left, right, and centre. I was flabbergasted! This was so new to me. When I gave the altar call that night for salvation, half of the people came up to the front. I tried to correct them, saying, "No, no, you don't understand. This isn't an altar call for healing. It's an altar call for salvation."

No one left the front. They were all weeping. They weren't up at the front to get healed; they wanted to get saved. These were people who had never been to our church. They would say things like, "Something just told us we needed to be here..."

This started months of healing-revival meetings. I remember times when we would finish up our Sunday morning church, and people would already be waiting outside for the evening service to begin. It got to the point where we couldn't fit any more people in the building, so we got a sound system so those outside could hear. People would even climb the building next to ours, so they could watch healings take place through the windows.

I remember one time walking through the grocery store, and I heard a few young guys in the aisle next to me. One of them said to another, "You need to go to this one church here in town. People are getting healed!"

The other guy said, "I don't believe in that stuff. That preacher must just be doing something."

The teenager said back to him, "I didn't believe it either until I saw it. Believe me, that preacher isn't doing anything. He just stands there with his mouth open looking more surprised than anyone!"

Not too long after that, a board member from the United Church from down the street contacted me saying they wanted to meet with me. I didn't know what to expect from the meeting. In all honesty, I thought those on the board were going to ream me out for what we were experiencing. When we met up, the chairman said to me, "We've been praying for revival for years. We've been to your meetings, and we know God is answering our prayers. We have the biggest building in town. We want to offer to you the use of our building for your healing meetings, but there's one condition: we don't want you to ever try to give us even a penny. We just want to be a part of this revival."

When I shared this with our congregation the following week, several of them were furious. The Pentecostals hated that we were going to move the revival meetings over to the other building. They said, "This is a move of God only for our church. If you move it over there, no one will come. Even if they do come, nothing is going to happen."

Boy were they wrong.

When we moved the healing services, that United church building had cars lined up all the way down the road. In the building, people filled any open space they could find. It didn't matter if it was in the sanctuary or the basement. No matter where people were in the building, they were getting healed.

We went week after week doing this, and invites started coming for me to travel and speak. I could feel in my spirit that God wanted to take what He was doing abroad. The power of God wasn't for one church; it wasn't for one town. His heart was burning to touch and heal the masses.

I sat on a rock overlooking the lake near our home, and I began to talk to God. What was happening was so overwhelming and I wanted to process with Him. Gwen and I went from living a quiet life one week, and then all of a sudden everything was exploding. We also began experiencing spiritual warfare that we never knew existed. We quickly learned that often when all of heaven breaks out, all of hell tries to derail what God is doing.

While sitting upon this rock, I had a vision of the nation of Canada. I saw Canada from east to west; from north to south. I saw the nation in revival. I saw one thousand young people on the streets of Ottawa doing the work of God. I saw miracles and healings breaking out in the streets. I saw Parliament halting because of the power of God falling. I saw huge stadiums that hadn't even been built yet being filled with people encountering Holy Spirit. In that moment I knew two things. First, I knew that this is what God was going to do. Second, I knew that I would give the rest of my life for this. I would give my life to see revival in Canada.

The first invitations that came in for me to speak were from the United States. They were from major ministries, conferences, and churches but I knew I couldn't go. I needed to stay in Canada. I needed to sow into this nation. My feeling was this: the United States has so much happening, but Canada felt barren in a lot of ways. That needed to change, and I couldn't help but believe we played a part in God's plan.

I began holding regular healing meetings in three Eastern Ontario communities each week, and I would travel on the weekends to other parts of Canada to minister. We saw Jesus perform amazing miracles across the nation. As a result of what the Lord was doing, I ended up being asked to host a television show, which ended up being the top Christian television program throughout Canada for many years. It was an amazing tool to minister to people. Not only that, but it made people aware of what God was doing in our country. Thanks to our television program, when we arrived in a city to minister, it wasn't uncommon for a few thousand people to show up. We were on television throughout Canada for about thirty-five years. Gwen and I threw our lives into Canada in every way we knew how.

After several years of ministering across Canada, I remember one moment vividly. I had just finished ministering one evening in Winnipeg. It was an amazing evening. God was faithful to move and change lives. People were healed and saved. As I would normally do after I ministered, I sat in my hotel room to calm down. I would need to do this because I would be vibrating from what God did. In the quiet of my hotel room, God spoke to me.

Reflecting on what I had seen that evening, God said, "You haven't done what I've told you."

I was so confused. I replied, saying, "Did you see what happened tonight?"

God spoke back to me, saying, "North."

"North..." I thought to myself, pondering the word.

I quickly realized that if you are going to believe for God to reach Canada, you need to do more than just go from sea to sea. You need to go from the river to the ends of the earth. This led us to begin ministering in the Arctic, where I fell in love with the Inuit people. For close to fifty years we've been ministering in the north of Canada. Native people are much more sensitive to the supernatural than we are, so it was the supernatural power of God that bonded us together. Our vision was to see the fire of God spread throughout the Arctic circles.

I say all of that to say this: I've seen revival. I've tasted it. I've seen it in grand cities, but also in small communities. I've seen it shake people and completely transform them. I've seen it across a nation. Experiencing this spoils you. I mean that in the sense that you can't settle any longer for what is considered normal in the church. You can't help but believe for the big and grand. You start dreaming beyond Sunday mornings, to dreaming for generations and nations.

Something that greatly excites me is how God is using the younger generation. I see them rising up in our nation. I've found that the people who find it hardest to embrace a fresh move of God are those who have been a part of previous outpourings. I've witnessed many people who had been a part of moves of God—they had been in the thick of it—get hung up on the fact that when God shows up in a new way, it often doesn't look like it did in the past. They've camped out in the previous.

I believe God wants to lead us where we've never gone before. I've had people say to me, "Bill, you're a lot different now than you were in the 1970s." Thank God I am! Back then I had to have a three-piece suit, a spotlight, and an organ. I couldn't get away with that now. We need to keep growing and maturing. We need to keep in step with the new things God is doing. A lot of the younger ones God is raising up haven't been a part of the previous moves. I believe this is one of the reasons why God is calling them. They are wide open to whatever God wants. The younger generation is poised to lead right now. What thrills me about the younger men and women I'm seeing is that I see them pursuing Holy Spirit. I see them valuing Him. They aren't trying to use Him for their own gain. I see a purity and an innocence. They have integrity. Their marriages are solid. Their families are solid. They have boldness and fire. I'm cheering them on.

I've told a lot of people, saying, "Canada shall be saved." Unfortunately, many people don't believe that. Even plenty of preachers don't believe it. I've had preachers respond to me, saying, "A nation can't be saved. You can't expect Canada to be completely Christian."

Actually, we can.

God is looking for those who will ask Him for the nations as their inheritance (Psalm 2:8). We need to remember that revival isn't a sovereign thing. We often think that it is—some teach that it is—but it's not. In 2 Chronicles 7:14 the Lord says, "If My people who are called by My name will humble themselves, and pray and seek My face, and turn from their wicked ways, then I will hear from heaven, and will forgive their sin and heal their land."

I believe the healing of the land is up to us; it's up to the church. We have to rise up. We need to allow our faith to be large. God is looking for people who will believe for nations. He's looking for people who have "from sea to sea" faith.

God wants to breathe revival in your nation.

— Bill Prankard

CHARLIE SHAMP

Charlie Shamp is the co-founder and president of Destiny Encounters International. He is a sought-after international keynote speaker. He has been commissioned by heaven as a prophet to bring healing and revival in the nations. He has ministered both nationally and internationally with radical demonstrations of faith, seeing lives transformed through the power of the Holy Spirit. Through the Holy Spirit, God has used Charlie to motivate many to move beyond mediocrity and embrace excellence and greatness. Charlie's heart is to empower and equip the Body of Christ with supernatural insight regarding what God has to say about their destiny and how to advance the kingdom of God on the earth. Through his ministry, people all over the world have been brought to the sacred truth that in Christ they are no longer victims, but overcomers in this life.

"One touch from the King changes everything. When you get touched by God tangibly, it will mark your life; and what you are marked with, you will be able to give to others."

— *Charlie Shamp*

Supernatural Hunger
By: Charlie Shamp

Over the years, I've learned that supernatural hunger drives the intensity of revival. We can't only live off of what God has done in the past. We can be thankful for what God has done in the past, but our hunger needs to push us to press into the greater things of the kingdom. God wants to pour out on the earth; He is simply looking for those who will partner with Him by having radical hunger.

In 2016, we saw a remarkable move of revival in Seattle. It began when a man named Darren Stott reached out to me, asking me to speak at his church. Darren is now one of my dearest friends; however, at the time I didn't know him. As a pastor, he felt that people in his church were very hungry for a move of the Spirit. He also felt I needed to deposit something that was going to impact the region.

At this time in my life, I had been experiencing an increase of the presence of God showing up in our meetings. Healings, signs, and wonders were taking place everywhere I went. It was hard to know how long a conference would last, because God was showing up so significantly. All that said, it was hard to pin down my schedule.

When Darren invited me to speak in Seattle, I remember saying to him, "I really want to come to your church. The thing is, my meetings have been really crazy, so it's hard for me to definitively commit to being somewhere. If I'm able to make it to Seattle, let's believe that God does something amazing."

More and more, I could feel that God wanted me in Seattle. Thankfully, it worked out for me to be there at a conference called "Declaration." The conference went smoothly; it was well attended. You could tell that the presence of God was increasing throughout the weekend, which I was happy about. By Sunday morning, the conference was coming to a close; but God had something else in store. I remember stepping into the sanctuary Sunday morning and there was a unique hunger for God in the room. It was tangible. It was the type of hunger that could move heaven. I began ministering on the miraculous. When I gave the altar call for people who were hungry for more of God, literally every person came up to the front. I looked at Darren; we both knew something was happening.

I felt like the Lord said that He wanted to release supernatural miracles in people's lives. As I prayed and moved in declaration, there was a woman in the meeting who I will never forget. She was in the side aisle of the sanctuary weeping uncontrollably, laying on her side. My wife, Brynn Leigh, noticed that something unique was happening to this lady and told me to find out what was taking place. We called this woman to the front and she shared about a creative miracle that she had just experienced. She shared how she once had breast cancer. Due to the cancer, the only way to save her life was to have her entire breast surgically removed. With tears streaming down her face, she testified that in that very meeting, her breast literally grew back!

This miracle was significant for this woman; it was significant for this church and everyone there. However, what no one knew, what that this miracle was very significant for me as well.

Over a decade before this church meeting took place, I had gone to Uganda. I met with a man of God who was known for bringing Pentecost to that particular country. He's a spiritual father to me. Over and over again, he saw this exact same miracle happening in his meetings. Women who had lost their breasts due to cancer would be completely healed and restored. Everywhere he went, he would see this creative miracle.

When I was only twenty years old, this man prophesied over me, saying, "Your ministry will significantly change, and you will move into more of a revival type of ministry when you see this miracle take place."

Here I am now at this conference in my thirties, over a decade later. I had finally witnessed the miracle he had prophesied about. The room was in chaos from what the Lord had done. I knew that something had dramatically shifted in my life.

After experiencing God pouring out in many meetings, I've learned that it's wise to be very cautious doing extended meetings. However, considering what had happened and after chatting with Darren, we felt we should extend the conference to see what would happen. We made an announcement that we would be meeting again that Sunday evening.

When we went to the church that night, the atmosphere was charged. It didn't feel like a conference or just another meeting; there was something special in the atmosphere. That night everything exploded. The presence of God came and people were laid out everywhere. The sound of revival came. There was weeping; there was laughing. There was screaming and shouting. It was electric.

We didn't know how long this would last, but we knew we couldn't stop. I ended up being in Seattle at this church for six solid weeks of revival. Every night, we didn't know what was going to happen. These nights were never about the messages; they were always about the presence of God. Going into these meetings, we would do what I would call "getting in the river." We would get into the atmosphere of those meetings and follow the Holy Spirit. We would get into the atmosphere of what God was doing in the room, and the messages would just flow. The preaching was spontaneous. I would sometimes wait in the presence of God for four or five hours before going to those services. We were fasting and praying, but there was never a pre-determined sermon. I would just wait for hours and the presence of God would come in. It would come crashing in like a wave, and we would just ride that wave the entire night. Sometimes the Holy Spirit would focus on deliverance; other times it would be healing. Sometimes the focus would be prophecy; other times it would be signs and wonders. No matter how He came, lives were being transformed.

We began doing water baptisms because there were so many people getting saved. In my opinion, those meetings became the most powerful ones. We had people come out who had been addicted to cocaine and meth for over fifteen years, and they would get instantly delivered when they were baptized. Some would get hit so hard by the presence of God while getting baptized that we would literally need to drag them out. People who were suicidal and depressed were completely delivered. There were so many miracles that took place. People who had dementia were coming into their right mind again. We saw remarkable signs and wonders. People would get gold crowns on their teeth during the services. Their dentists would be astounded when these people went in for check-ups. Oil from heaven would pour out of people's hands. The altar calls for salvation were consistent every night. There were even drug dealers and witches who would come into the church and they would get saved!

The joy of God was another significant part of the meetings. People would literally have to be carried out of the buildings, and then couldn't even drive home because of the joy of the Lord impacting them. Some might wonder, "Is this normal for these people? Are these the type of people who experience this all the time?" To be honest, a lot of the ones getting dramatically impacted by God were those who had just heard about the revival spontaneously. I'll give you an example:

There was one lady who lived by the church. One day while driving home, she said she felt like she drove into a wall of sorts when passing by the church. It was a wall made of something she couldn't explain. She said she felt compelled to come in.

During the service, this woman sat in the back. I didn't know what had happened to her while driving past the church. I felt like God was highlighting her to me. From the stage, I said, "God is doing something to you right now. Can you step out into the aisle?"

She came out into the aisle and I began calling out some words of knowledge for what she needed healing from. I said, "The power of God is going to hit you right now. Receive it!"

What happened next still rocks me to my core. We even have this on film. Right when I said to her, "Receive it!" You can see on the video an orb that comes out of nowhere. This orb hit her and she fell right over, instantly delivered and healed. This was a woman who had never experienced anything like this before in her life.

I've learned that hunger drives the intensity of revival. Something happens when we are no longer satisfied with what we have experienced in the past, spurring us to pursue the *more*. Not long before I was in Seattle, I was at another church. The power of God came into that meeting with such force that I couldn't even get off the floor for two and a half hours. I knew that God wanted to do something profound in this place. The same power that would show up in Seattle was in this place.

When I went down to lay upon the floor in the presence of God, I invited everyone up to the front, saying, "The Lord's doing something. I can't preach right now, but feel free to come up to the front to partake of what God is doing."

As I said, the same presence that was in Seattle had shown up in this church, but something was different: the people didn't respond to the presence of God. They didn't respond to what He was doing. God wanted to move, but because people weren't stirring up their hunger, there was a moment that was missed. We can see from this story how crucial it is for us to partner with God in our hunger.

A few years ago, I was in Australia. There were less than one hundred people in the meeting, but I could feel their hunger. During the service, I got caught up in a trance and literally could not move. The power of God blew right in. Many people were touched.

The host of the conference said to me after this conference, "That was incredible. What do you think we should do?"

I said, "I think we should have another meeting."

She said, "Are you sure?"

I said, "Yes. I feel like there is an opportunity for us to press into something. I felt the presence of revival. I know the feeling and I know the sound; I know it's here."

We had another meeting that night. A girl came who had previously tried to commit suicide. She had tried jumping off a building and her neck was broken. Thankfully she survived; but she was bound to a wheelchair. In that meeting, the power of God came in and she stood up and began walking!

That one miracle made everything explode. I actually had to cancel other speaking engagements in order to stay and help steward what God was doing. When this moment of outpouring comes, there is an incredible cost. We need to be hungry enough to pay that cost. I've had times where I've been booked with speaking engagements, but when revival shows up, I need to adjust. I've had to do this many times. Not everyone likes that, but I never regret it. I don't regret it because of the miracles we've seen and because of the souls that were saved.

In only a few nights, we watched as this group of less than one hundred people grew to almost seven hundred fifty people. It got to the point where we needed to change facilities five different times because of the size of the crowds. We saw people giving their lives to Jesus every single night. People think revival has to do with the building, but that's not true. It has nothing to do with the building. It has to do with the people and the hunger.

I believe we are called to carry revival. I do believe that revival can be sovereign, but I also believe that God wants to use people to usher it in. Therefore, we have a choice in whether or not we will come under submission to the will of heaven. If we are hungry to be used, God will use us. When He comes, we need to be willing to go with Him. We can't continue on with the program we had planned. We have to let it all go to the wind if need be. Revival is more important than our schedule. We can't expect heaven to submit to our schedule; we need to be willing to adjust our lives to what God is doing.

I believe there is a tenacity for those who carry revival. This tenacity allows them to be able to go into any atmosphere and see the miraculous. Over the years, we've taken teams to dark places. We've taken teams into places to do evangelism, and when we leave we will hear of people being shot and killed on those same streets where we were witnessing to people. It may sound extreme that we do this, but I liken it to what the Salvation Army did. William Boothe would go down to riots, brothels, and bars. They would see Jesus move in the most unlikely of places, but the reality is that in those dark places there are people who are very precious to God. He wants to meet with them. He wants to set them free.

One time, we walked up to a few kids who were doing drugs on the side of the street. One of the boys had been deaf ever since he was born. We prayed for him, and God opened his ear right on the spot. His friends were blown away! All of them decided to give their lives to Jesus right then and there. This wasn't in the church. This happened in the dark places.

We need to remember the heart of revival. Revival is about winning the lost. It's about Jesus reaching into what seem like impossible situations to prove His goodness and love.

I was ministering at a church a few years ago. I won't share where it was or the church's name. While speaking, the power of God blew in. I gave an altar call at the end and there must have been three hundred people who came up to the front to receive Jesus. Three hundred people were born again right in that moment! People were getting blasted everywhere. Some were falling out of their chairs; some were weeping. Joy was hitting people. Demons were leaving people. It was crazy!

I went to lunch the next day with the pastor. He said to me, "We really enjoyed the meeting last night. We feel that tonight is going to be the last night and we aren't going to extend the meetings."

I asked him, saying, "Why? Three hundred people were born again last night."

He said, "I know. We feel that these have been good meetings, but we aren't going to extend."

I said, "Okay, I'll honour your decision. Tonight can be the last meeting."

I was spending time with the Lord before that meeting and He spoke so clearly to me. He said, "I'm going to do something mind-blowing and significant in this meeting. When I do this, whatever you do, do not extend these meetings. I'm going to show you the hearts of people."

"Okay, Lord," I complied.

I went into the meeting that night and God was true to His word; He did something mind-blowing. During the meeting, an angel came right into the sanctuary. From head to toe, this angel was covered in gold. It went right over top of the people who were sitting. At that time, my son who was in this meeting with me was eating a bag of popcorn. This angel went over top of him and covered him in gold flakes. The thing is that not only was he covered, but also his popcorn! This took place in front of everyone. As the service went on, people started getting supernatural oil on their hands. Signs and wonders were happening all over the place.

At one point in the meeting, a man ran up to the front who had never been in a church service before in his life.

He said, "A miracle just happened! It has to do with my bank account!"

"What about your bank account?" I asked.

He said, "I just got $5522.14 put into my bank account from nowhere! I just came... I need to give my life to Jesus right now!"

He and his wife both gave their lives to Jesus that night. I was absolutely blown away by everything God was doing.

Once the service wrapped up, I was curious to see how the pastor was going to reply.

He came up to me, saying, "I really feel like we need to extend the meetings now."

I knew what God had said to me; He didn't want the meetings to be extended. "No, we are not extending," I replied.

The pastor said, "I think you're going to miss God then."

I said, "You already missed Him, because you care more about the signs and wonders than you do about the saving of souls."

I then said, "I refuse to build anything off of signs and wonders. I don't build anything this way. Revival is about the changing of the soul. So, we're not extending."

I share this story because we need to be very careful in how we build revival. God watches how we build. It's true that some of the key indicators of true revival are miracles, signs, and wonders; but you know without a doubt that revival is taking place when there is significant change happening in people's souls and lives. We know revival is occurring when people are genuinely getting saved and are completely changing their lives. We need to keep our focus on the right things. Is heaven excited when signs and wonders take place? Absolutely. However, do you know what gets heaven really excited? When people are born again.

God wants to position us to receive a touch from Him. He wants to give each of us the true heart of revival. He wants to mark us with supernatural hunger. He wants to mark us with boldness. He wants to mark us with a burden and desire to see people saved.

Many people care about having a flourishing ministry, but ministries will come and go. Revivalists will always be remembered; people who change culture will always be remembered. That said, having a great ministry shouldn't be the end goal. We need to want to see true transformation and change. We need to have a heart to truly be vessels of revival.

One touch from the King changes everything. When we get in the presence of God and we begin to go after Him with hunger and desperation, He will come and touch us. What He touches us with, we will be able to transfer to others. The touch of God is transferable and it's real. It can change hearts. It can change regions. It can change nations.

All of the kingdom generals we commemorate throughout history were people just like you and me. The thing that set them apart was that they had the touch of God on their lives.

When we seek God, we will be able to do the same.

— Charlie Shamp

REVIVAL COMMISSIONING

We are living in times of revival. God is encountering hearts throughout the earth. He is healing the sick. He is freeing the oppressed. He is transforming cities. He is shaking nations. He is marking generations.

Throughout this book, you've read stories of revival. You've read testimonies of God using individuals to transform hearts, heal bodies, and see the oppressed set free. You've heard stories of how God has used men and women to influence culture, shake nations, and mark generations. You've heard keys that fathers and mothers of the faith have learned for seeing God move in and through them. What you need to realize is that chapter by chapter, story by story, you've been receiving an impartation from heaven. You've been receiving an impartation of revival.

Our prayer is that these stories won't only be something that you know in your head, but that they will be written on your heart as well. Our desire is that these would be stories that you not only remember, but that you also live out in your life. Our prayer is that they will make you hungry for the deep things of God; that they will mark you. We pray that you would have a burden and desire to see revival in all facets of your life. Our heart is that you will never settle for less than who you were created to be; that you won't be able to help but rise up in faith and believe for what others deem to be impossible.

Some of you reading might be in conventional ministry, while others are in business or government. Some of you might be in the arts and entertainment, media, or the education system, while others might be called to family or the health care system. No matter where you are called, God wants to use you to bring healing, freedom, and transformation. He wants you to stand as one who marks your sphere of influence with heaven.

You were made for revival. You were made for the extravagant and the remarkable. You were made to be a bridge for heaven to invade earth; for the Father heart of God to impact hearts and lives. No matter where you are called, no matter what background you've come out of, you are a voice of revival.

As you've read all of the stories throughout this book, you'll notice that they are all different. They are all unique; but they are born of the same Spirit. Just like every person has their own distinct fingerprint, everyone has a distinct voice. Your voice is unique. Your voice matters today. God wants you to discover that voice. Now is your opportunity to dive into what God has for you, to explore the uniqueness of your voice; the uniqueness of your calling, knowing that there is no one like you.

Revival isn't for a select group of people; it's an invitation for all who will believe. God is looking for someone just like you who will be courageous enough to rise in faith; to believe.

You are now a carrier of these stories. You are a carrier of these revelations, keys, and secrets. Now, it is time for you to write your story.

We want to pray a prayer with you. As you read these words, don't simply read them; but let them sink into your heart. Let God's presence consume you.

"Father, I thank you for all of those who have gone before me and have shown me what is possible for those who believe. You have called me for such a time as this. I lay down any mentality of lack that would prevent me from dreaming with You. I lay down any doubt that would prevent me from believing for the remarkable to be seen through my life. I trade in lack for legacy. I trade in doubt for faith. Father, I ask you to give me a revelation of who I truly am and what I carry. I thank you that I am a voice of revival. Show me the importance of my voice. Teach me how to use it to bring healing, hope, and revival. Raise me up to be a beacon of light in dark places. Use me to heal and transform culture. Use me to impact hearts with Your love. Use me to be a signpost, pointing people to You. Let my life be one of legacy, that I would leave an inheritance to those who will come after me. Mark me with your love. Mark me with faith. Mark me with revival.

I pray all of this in Jesus' name. Amen."

It is time to write your story. God has called you to be a voice of revival in your generation.